Comic Con
Conversations

BearManor
Media

Orlando, Florida

Published in the USA by
BearManor Media
1317 Edgewater Dr. #110
Orlando, FL 32804
www.BearManorMedia.com

Softcover Edition
ISBN-10:
ISBN-13: 978-1-62933-922-1

Printed in the United States of America

Introduction

Invariably whenever Jason and I do a new book, someone asks why we chose the topic that we did. With respect to the book in your hands, the answer is quite easy.

It was the only one of our brilliant ideas that the publisher was interested in, and it immediately became our favorite because we are a couple of whores.

Plus, it is one of our favorite topics. Fan conventions are an absolute blast, whether we are at them as celebrity guests, vendors or just plain fans. It is an opportunity for us to mingle with real comic pros, celebrities and other fans.

It is also a good chance to spend quality time with our wives, who come along to make sure we aren't spending the next three mortgage payments on stuff we didn't know we needed in order to live until we saw it.

Whether you go to a small show with a couple of hundred people attending or a big multi-day show drawing more than a hundred thousand fans, you will have fun. If you want to cosplay, go for it. If you want to go leer at female cosplayers, pray you can outrun me, you disgusting little bastard.

The best endorsement I can think of for fan conventions is the experience of my mother. At the age of 79 and 11 months, she went to her first show as a courtesy to me, and had a great time listening to panels and looking at costumes. I knew she truly had a great time when, at her 80th birthday party, she was trying to convince a couple of her friends from her senior's apartment complex to go to the show next year with her.

It should be noted that this book was more than five years in the making, and was delayed in part by the global pandemic which basically put an end to fan conventions for a while. Some of the references may seem dated, but are hopefully still enjoyable and will make you want to go to fan conventions.

Betsy Baker

Betsy Baker was born in Cedar Rapids, Iowa - a middle child - and grew up in St. Joseph, Michigan. She started piano lessons at the age of five and also took voice lessons and studied dance. She attended Michigan State University and graduated with a degree in theater education and classical voice. After graduating, Baker embarked upon headline engagements throughout the south, including The Eden Roc in Miami Beach, Florida and other venues, with a group called Musicana. Betsy eventually found herself in Detroit, where she honed her craft in television, radio voice-overs and industrial films. Baker landed the role of Linda in the film *The Evil Dead* after she came to Sam Raimi's attention in Detroit.

Can you give us a quick list of the fan conventions you have appeared at, as both a fan and celebrity guest?

I have not attended any conventions as a fan. As part of "The Ladies of The Evil Dead," we have attended numerous conventions in the U.S., Canada, and Europe for the last 18 years – Chiller, MonsterMania, Horrorfest, ComicCon, Cinema Wasteland, Creation Entertainment, to name just a few.

What is the strangest thing you have been asked to autograph?
The upper most region of a man's thigh…. right underneath a large tattoo of a picture of The Ladies of Evil Dead.

What is the most inappropriate thing a fan has done or said to you?
A marriage proposal.

What about the flipside? What is the sweetest or most touching thing a fan has said or done for you?
People have brought us artwork that they have created as a gift of appreciation. That's really nice.

Have you had people come up to you dressed as one of your characters?
All the time! - It's especially fun to see 'us' at a costume party during the convention.

When I was at the Calgary comic book convention, a 400 pound guy stepped on my foot and I yelled out "Jesus Christ!" A cosplayer dressed as Jesus Christ (at least I think it was a cosplayer) promptly appeared and offered to heal me. What is your personal WTF story from any convention?
Well, I've never had Jesus Christ come by the table. That's impressive.

What experiences have you had with fans who know far more about your career than you could ever hope to know? How do you deal with that situation?
I'm intrigued and impressed with fans who know my films, my TV work and my commercials. They sometimes remind me of some of the work I did that I had forgotten!

Have you ever been mistaken for someone else at a convention, and thought "why the Hell did you think I was them?"
Betsy Palmer. Same first name, wrong person. Sorry to disappoint.

You have been photographed thousands of times. What is your favorite photo with a fan, and what was the one request that made you shake your head, laugh or throw up a little in your mouth?

There is usually an odd request at every convention we've attended. I've been asked to take a picture with a fan while I was eating in a restaurant. Can I please just chew first?

Before you became a celebrity you were a fan. Ever have any true fangirl moments encountering celebrities before you became one?

I wrote a letter to Richard Chamberlin ("Dr. Kildare") when I was eight years old. I wanted to be on his show – dying, and I wanted him to save me. He sent me an 8X10 picture but he didn't invite me onto the show. Darn.

You have been interviewed and done panels at conventions. What are the funniest, strangest and most thought-provoking questions you have encountered?

Where do I begin?

Have you done any foreign conventions yet?

Yes – various cons in Germany, UK, and Canada.

You are constantly on the road. What is the hardest part about travel, and your funniest story from being on the road?

Not constantly – occasionally. One time I worked on a TV show, took a red-eye to a convention on the east coast, washed my face, brushed my teeth, and changed my clothes in an airport restroom, took the next leg of the trip to be picked up and driven directly to the convention where I sat down at a table, had some coffee, signed, and got on the plane the next morning at 7 am to fly back home.

OK, now it's all you: What is the one knock-'em-dead, blow-their-socks-off fan convention story that you haven't told us yet? It can be funny, sad, scary, sexy, heart-warming, terrifying, sexy, action packed, cerebral, sexy or gross. Did I mention it could be sexy?

We have attended a few weddings that took place during the convention... themed accordingly.... In a hotel lobby or meeting room. Different – but it's what the bride and groom wanted!!

Belinda Balaski

Belinda Belaski in (clockwise from upper left) *Cannonball, Bobbi Jo and the Outlaw, The Howling,* and in real life.

Belinda Belaski's amazing career began when she was five and continues to this day. Among her many accomplishments is an Emmy win (and two other Emmy nominations), and appearing in 11 Joe Dante films, the most recent being *Nightmare Cinema* in 2018. She is a true horror icon, having had key roles in *Piranha*, *The Howling*, and, perhaps most famously, in cult director Bert I. Gordon's *Food of the Gods*.

She prides herself on being a character actress, and has transformed herself from everything from the Tuesday-Wells-type surfer girl in *Cannonball* to the small-town friend of Lynda Carter in *Bobbi Jo and the Outlaw*.

Besides appearing at The Hollywood Show, Belinda loves appearing at horror-themed conventions and describes the fans she has met there as the best people in the world. If you get a chance, go and meet this incredibly charming and talented actress.

And if you have a *Gremlins* poster, have her sign it. Trust me.

Can you give us a quick list of the fan conventions you have appeared at as a celebrity guest?
The Hollywood Show, Cinema Wasteland, Monsterpalooza, Horror Hound, Monster Mania and many other horror conventions. I love horror conventions. They are so rewarding.

What is the strangest thing you have been asked to autograph?
Stuffed Gizmos. There is no place to sign Gizmo. He's all hair. I prefer it when fans bring a *Gremlins* poster to be signed. I always sign on Zach Galligan's fly.

What is the most inappropriate thing a fan has done or said to you?
Dee Wallace and I were appearing at the same show and a fan came running up "Dee Wallace! Dee Wallace!" and then they looked at me and said "Are you her assistant?" Dee got angry with them and said, "I can't believe you just said that! She starred with me in *The Howling*!" Love that girl!

What about the flipside? What is the sweetest or most touching thing a fan has said or done for you?

Everybody is so nice at horror conventions. I'm always shocked when people come up to me reciting my dialogue from movies. Sometimes I have to say, "Oh, was that me?" Actors can't remember every word of dialogue they have ever said. Oh, and to answer your question, I have had grown men come up to me and say that when they saw my death scene in *Piranha* when they were younger they cried. It is sweet to know that you have touched someone in that way. It says a lot about how your fans love you.

Actually because of that death scene, John Sayles actually created a character for me in *The Howling*. My character Terry does not appear in the book, but my character in *Piranha* inspired him to create the part for me.

Have you had people come up to you dressed as one of your characters?
Never. My characters usually dress very ordinary. In shooting *The Howling*, I wore the same blue blazer, jeans and Nikes for four and a half months.

When I was at the Calgary comic book convention, a 400 pound guy stepped on my foot and I yelled out "Jesus Christ!" A cosplayer dressed as Jesus Christ (at least I think it was a cosplayer) promptly appeared and offered to heal me. What is your personal WTF story from any convention?
I was one of about thirty actors who were flown over to Germany for one convention. We were all given guarantees to appear. It turned out the promoter and her husband had just split up and he organized a convention for the same weekend as hers. About ten people showed up for our show. After the show, the promoter organized a meeting for all of the actors. This woman who was perfectly fluent in English suddenly couldn't speak or understand English and showed up with an interpreter who said none of us could be paid immediately. She broke down and was sobbing and crying. We all agreed to defer payment. I agreed that I didn't have to be paid until Christmas. None of us ever saw a dime. She lives in a different country, so what can we do? We can't sue her. I have since learned that she has pulled the exact same act with the same interpreter and the same crying routine four other times.

At another show, I won't say where, my agent told me at the show that there was no money to pay anyone. I put my boots on and marched over to the office of the people running the show and demanded they pay me. They said nobody was getting paid because they made no money. I said if they made no money, they could just empty their pockets onto the table and I would take whatever they had. Suddenly one of them pulls out a thick wad of bills, peels off what I was owed, and shoves the rest of it back in his pocket.

Dee Wallace and I were doing a show in Texas and they weren't going to pay what they owed us. They said they only had a thousand dollars and they would give us each five hundred. Dee wanted the whole thousand. I don't blame her and I'm not mad at her because we all have mortgages to meet and bills to pay, right? They ended up giving us five hundred each then and the rest later. I got paid in full for that one.

You have been an actor for 40 years. What experiences have you had with fans who know far more about your career than you could ever hope to know? How do you deal with that situation?

Generally, I love fans like that, except when they want to talk about my first movie, the one I wish nobody had ever seen. It's usually shown at 4:00 a.m. I wore a cheap wig and my co-star was very clumsy and every time he put his arm around me you can see my wig go up and down. I refuse to tell you the name of the movie.

What other celebrity encounters have you had at conventions? Feel free to tell us any funny, sexy and/or terrifying close encounters you have had.

Everyone is so wonderful except the ones with the really big egos and the big guarantees who charge $100 an autograph and stay in the hotel penthouse. People like that never mix with the other guests. However, I love it when I run into people I worked with years ago. I ran into Meg Foster at The Hollywood Show. We hadn't seen each other since we had both appeared in *Baretta*. She is amazing. At another show I ran into Cloris Leachman. We did *Death Scream* and *Mrs. R's Daughter* together and she is just a riot. She recognized me immediately and said, "How are you, dear?" I had interrupted her signing a photo. She had just written her first name and then looked up at her assistant like 'what am I writing', so her assistant said, "Leachman". Everyone laughed.

I appeared at the same show as Keir Dullea once. I am a big fan of his. Everyone knows him for *2001: A Space Odyssey*, but I loved him in *Bunny Lake is Missing* and *David and Lisa*. I actually had someone go get his autograph for me and tell him how much I loved him in that film.

My worst experience was with Mickey Rooney. My dad was a very well-known jockey and he rode horses owned by Mickey Rooney in the 1940's. There are pictures of him and my dad together. My dad won a lot of money for him. My mom said if I ever had a chance I should talk to him because he loved my dad. We were appearing at the same show so I stood in line with everyone else even though I had on a celebrity guest ribbon. I finally got up to see him and told him how he had known my dad. He gave me a very unimpressed "Yeah?" I showed him a picture of him and my dad together and he just said, "What?" Then he waved his hand to tell me to go away. I can somewhat sympathize with him now, because it can be hard when someone you don't know starts talking about something out of context, and I know I'm making excuses for someone but I know how hard it is when you are trying to be in the moment and people start talking about the past.

Have you ever been mistaken for someone else at a convention, and thought "why the Hell did you think I was them?"
Mainly Patty Duke, but also Cloris Leachman and Lee Remick. People say I have Lee Remick's eyes, but mostly I get Patty Duke.

Cosplay has become an art form. What costume at any convention has totally blown you away and amazed you with its high quality and detail? What is the all-time worst costume you have seen?
When I first started doing conventions, I thought it was like a zoo. People would come up covered in tattoos and piercings and I thought it was a costume but it was just how they looked. It was like something out of Melrose Street, which is a punk street in Los Angeles. Then they open their mouths and they are the kindest, sweetest, most respectful people you have ever met.

The absolute best costumes are when there are professional special effects artists actually at the show to work on the fans. At Monsterpalooza they have a whole room of special effects people and they work on the fans and also have models walking around that they have done. It is amazing. They really honor special effects artists at that show. I just did a movie called *Nightmare Cinema*. Joe Dante directed the segment I'm in. Howard Berger who has won an Emmy for makeup on *The Walking Dead* did my makeup. I spent eight hours a day in the chair. You WON'T recognize me... not even my voice.... At Monsterpalooza, that is the same quality of makeup you are going to see.

Whenever someone makes their own costume, it is great. It gives them a way to honor the superheroes and characters they love. I'm an actor. I've played dress-up for more than forty years. To me, the only bad costumes are the ones that are way too risqué.

You have been photographed thousands of times. What is your favorite photo with a fan, and what was the one request that made you shake your head, laugh or throw up a little in your mouth?

My all-time favorite photo is one of me and John Landis at a show. We were just sitting and talking and people started snapping our picture, and I had one of them give me a copy. I mean there I was with John Landis!!!

Before you became a celebrity you were a fan. Ever have any true fan moments encountering celebrities before you became one?

My mom used to take me to the race track whenever my dad was riding. In those days it really was the sport of kings. When I was five, my best friend was Jimmy Durante. Whenever he saw me, he would say, "There's my best friend!" and pick me up and hug me. I never realized he was an actor. One day I saw him on TV calling someone else his best friend and I was furious. I was totally devastated. I cried and cried. The next time I saw him I crossed my arms and wouldn't talk to him. My mom told him what happened and he said, "Oh no, you really *ARE* my best friend!" Race tracks were magical places in those days with friends of my parents like Betty Grable & Harry James, Lucy & Desi Arnez, Bing Crosby (my Dad rode for Crosby & Lin Howard Stables), Mickey, everybody was there, dressed to the 10's! It was such an incredible time to be on the track! However, my father was killed in a race in 1965 and I've just never been able to go back.

My mom was a singer and was best friends with Betty Grable and knew Harry James, as she was singing with the big bands in Lexington, Kentucky when Dad went there to ride in the Derby. That is how they met.

You have been interviewed and done panels at conventions. What are the funniest, strangest and most thought provoking questions you have encountered?

I was doing a Q and A with Dee Wallace, Kelli Maroney, the twins from *The Shining*, and Margot Kidder. It was the first time I ever met Margot. She is truly a real funny, earthy person. Each of us was asked a question and I was asked when did I first know that *The Howling & Piranha,* and these films that I was in were considered classics. I thought about it a second and said, "Facebook?" The entire room dropped with laughter! But really it's true, until there was Facebook I had no idea that there were such devoted fans or that anyone really even saw our films! Along with these amazing conventions! The proof is surely in the pudding!!!

Have you done any foreign conventions yet?
Only the German one. Never again unless I am paid in front.

You are constantly on the road. What is the hardest part about travel, and your funniest story from being on the road?
When I was a kid, we moved every three months because my dad was a jockey and we had to be where horse racing was in season. I've been on the road all my life. Whenever I make a movie it means being away from home for months.

The worst part of travel is airports. They used to be fun, but now with all of the security measures they are awful places.

It's not funny at the time, but the funniest ones are probably when I am supposed to be on the road but I'm not, like waking up in Los Angeles at 8 when I was supposed to be on set in Las Vegas at 7. That's when I was frantically calling my agent to say I was on my way.

Now it's all you: What is the one knock-'em-dead, blow-their-socks-off fan convention story that you haven't told us yet? It can be funny, sad, scary, sexy, heart-warming, terrifying, sexy, action packed, cerebral, sexy or gross. Did I mention it could be sexy? I'm trying to sell some books here.
It's actually an audition story, but it is funny. I was in my twenties and my agent said there were these two new directors who were looking for

someone to play teenagers. They each had a different project but they were interviewing together. I was still playing teenagers and went down with my book of photos. They were going through my photos, when the one guy George says, "You winked at me." I said I hadn't, but he insisted. He asks the other director, a guy named Brian, who said he didn't know. I stood up and grabbed my photos and told them they were just looking to play around and I was only interested in working.

George was George Lucas and he was looking for someone to play Princess Leia in *Star Wars*. Brian De Palma was the other guy and he was casting *Carrie*.

I always say that if I ever meet George Lucas again, I am definitely winking at him.

I HAVE KNOWN BERT I. GORDON FOR YEARS. I STILL SEE HIM AT CONVENTIONS AND HE IS ENTHUSIASTIC AS EVER AND LOOKS THE SAME AS HE DID 40 YEARS AGO, EVEN THOUGH HE IS IN HIS 90S.

RATS, BELINDA. THE KEY IS TO KEEP THINKING *"RATS"*

WHEN HE DIRECTED ME IN THE GIANT RAT MOVIE FOOD OF THE GODS, HE TRIED TO GIVE EVERYONE THE PROPER MOTIVATION

WE FILMED ON AN ISLAND OFF THE COAST OF BRITISH COLUMBIA. IT HAD THE GREY, DISMAL LOOK THAT BERT WANTED FOR THE MOVIE. IT WAS PERFECT.

AND THEN IT STARTED TO SNOW AND IT WOULDN'T STOP OR MELT.

ONLY BERT I. GORDON WOULD TRY TO DIRECT MOTHER NATURE.

IT WENT ON FOR DAYS. IDA LUPINO WENT SO FAR AS TO WRITE A DEATH SCENE FOR HER CHARACTER SO SHE COULD GO BACK HOME. INSTEAD, BERT TRIED TO TAKE MATTERS INTO HIS OWN HANDS.

WHEN I WAS IN JOE DANTE'S WEREWOLF MOVIE THE HOWLING, THE WEREWOLF HAD NOT BEEN CONSTRUCTED YET, SO WE HAD TO ACT AS IF WE WERE TERRIFIED OF THIN AIR.

I WENT BACK TO HAWAII, AND FOUR AND A HALF MONTHS LATER I GOT THE CALL THAT THE WEREWOLF FOOTAGE WAS DONE AND WE COULD DO THE SHOTS THAT INVOLVED THAT ACTORS IN THE SAME SCENE AS IT

I EXPLAINED THAT MY HAIR HAD GROWN OUT OVER TWO INCHES SINCE WE LAST FILMED, BUT I WAS ASSURED IT WAS NOT A PROBLEM BECAUSE I STILL LOOKED THE SAME AS WHEN THE OTHER SCENES WERE FILMED

NOT A PROBLEM

SO, IF YOU WATCH THE HOWLING TODAY IN SLOW MOTION, YOU WILL SEE MY CHARACTER EXPERIENCE THE FASTEST HAIR GROWTH IN HOLLYWOOD HISTORY

I APPEARED IN THE "ROAST YOUR LOVED ONE" SEGMENT DIRECTED BY JOE DANTE IN AMAZON WOMEN ON THE MOON, WHICH WAS ABOUT A FUNERAL DONE IN THE FORM OF A HOLLYWOOD ROAST.

COMEDIANS LIKE HENNY YOUNGMAN, JACKIE VERNON, SLAPPY WHITE, CHARLIE CALLAS AND RIP TAYLOR PLAYED THEMSELVES, AND THEY ALL ROUTINELY PERFORMED AT REAL HOLLYWOOD ROASTS. I DIDN'T. THEY SPENT THE DAY GOOFING AROUND AND BEING HILARIOUS. IT WAS A LITTLE INTIMIDATING.

JOE DECIDED TO SHOOT BEFORE A LIVE AUDIENCE WITH FIVE CAMERA. WE HAD TO DO IT ALL IN ONE TAKE FOR IT TO WORK.

LEGENDARY TALK SHOW HOST STEVE ALLEN INTRODUCED MY CHARACTER AT THE ROAST.

THANK YOU, MERV.

I DECIDED THAT THE GUYS SHOULDN'T GET ALL OF THE LAUGHS. JOE KEPT MY AD LIB IN THE MOVIE.

I THINK POOR STEVE ALLEN WENT TO HIS GRAVE THINKING THAT I REALLY THOUGHT HE WAS MERV GRIFFIN.

WHEN I APPEARED ON THE A-TEAM, THE SEGMENT I WAS IN WAS SHOT OUTSIDE AND NOT ON THE SOUNDSTAGE WHERE MOST OF THE SHOW WAS SHOT.

MY CHARACTER WAS AN ITINERANT FARM WORKER, AND IT WAS 120 DEGREES OUTSIDE WHILE WE WERE FILMING WITH NO SHADE IN SIGHT.

AND THERE IN THE MIDDLE OF THE SCORCHING SUN, WAS MR. T. LIFTING WEIGHTS WHILE THE REST OF US WERE DYING OF HEAT STROKE.

ON THE ONE HAND IT WAS A GREAT SIGN OF HIS DEDICATION.

ON THE OTHER HAND I FELT LIKE GOING UP TO HIM AND SAYING

WHAT ARE YOU DOING? GO INTO YOUR TRAILER WHERE IT'S AIR CONDITIONED! GO HAVE LUNCH! YOU DON'T HAVE TO BE HERE!

BUT UNLESS IT WAS CALLED FOR IN A SCRIPT, NOBODY HAD THE GUTS TO TALK TO MR. T THAT WAY, PRESENT COMPANY INCLUDED.

Chris Bernhard

Can you give us a quick list of the fan conventions you have organized or attended?

I've attended Toronto Comic Con way back in 2000, various Vancouver Comic Shows from 2006-2008, Calgary Expo in 2006, 2007 and 2008. My business partner and I started the Saskatchewan Entertainment Expo in 2013 and have been running that show since then.

What is the strangest thing you have seen asked to be autographed?

Honestly, I don't really do the celebrity side of things, but I've heard of body parts getting signed so they can be tattooed.

What about the flipside? What is the sweetest or most touching thing a fan has said or done at one of your shows?

We get so many positive comments about our volunteer crew and how vital and important they are to the experience.

You interact with fans and vendors at conventions. What is the strangest thing someone has tried to sell at one of your shows?

We had a fortune teller once that lasted a sum total of 2 hours. She got very discouraged that no one was buying palm readings from her.

Your show features celebrities from different media and genres. How do fans of different sub-genres interact with each other? Have you seen any funny or shocking confrontations between fans over the years?

None whatsoever, everyone really gets along.

When I was at the Calgary comic book convention, a 400 pound guy stepped on my foot and I yelled out "Jesus Christ!" A cosplayer dressed as Jesus Christ (at least I think it was a cosplayer) promptly appeared and offered to heal me. What is your personal WTF story from any convention?

Honestly, I don't have one. Most of the shows I attended as a fan didn't have cosplay as an element at the show; it was just people purchasing comics, art and getting autographs from celebrities. As an organizer, I'm busy making sure the show happens and trucks along reasonably, so I don't have a lot of time to interact and take in the action at the show.

What is your average convention attendee like, and which person really surprised you by being a fan?

I don't really think there are "average" fans - everyone is exceptional in their own way with the fandoms they love and respect. I've seen everything from 65-year-old grandfathers bringing their grandchildren, to 14-year-olds trying to bring their 7 years siblings to the show.

What about haters? Have people come to your conventions just to say how much they hate pop culture or your particular guests?

Sometimes. I don't understand it personally, but that's their prerogative, right?

Cosplay has become an art form. What costume at any convention has totally blown you away and amazed you with its high quality and detail? What is the all-time worst costume you have seen?

Hmmm - I saw this really great athletic Spiderman once that posed for people on garbage cans and he had really great balance. The suit was top notch.

Worst costume? I have no barometer as I don't really spend a lot of time checking out costumes.

What about stars who aren't convention regulars or are appearing at their first show? Are they surprised by how strong their fandom is? How do they react to their first conventions?

Shannon Purser was great and super excited to be at the show. She didn't have the biggest line, but you could tell that she was just so thankful.

Comic book conventions have gone from small gatherings to huge multi-media showcases. How has your show in particular changed and how has the type of celebrity who appears at them changed?

We started our show as an Entertainment Expo - so the change from Comic Book convention to something else didn't really happen with our show. We've just gotten larger and had a bigger physical footprint. We've had a number of guests at the show from all walks, TV, animation, movies so that hasn't really changed over time. We've always had a robust creator line up which I've heard is different time and time again because we are a smaller show in the grand scheme of things.

Photo ops are a convention favorite. Tell us about the more memorable ones you have seen.

I don't do photo ops either - I have heard stories about people getting engaged in a photo op though. That would likely be pretty special for the couple in the photo op.

Do you get many international fans at your shows, or fans of foreign pop culture?

Not really. We do get a few people that come to our show from the Northern U.S. but that is about it. I mean, do you consider Anime foreign pop culture? At this point, I don't. The lines are completely blurred.

OK, now it's all you: What is the one knock-'em-dead, blow-their-socks-off fan convention story that you haven't told us yet? It can be funny, sad, scary, sexy, heart-warming, terrifying, sexy, action packed, cerebral, sexy or gross. Did I mention it could be sexy?

I guess the best story I have is that our son, Bram, was born the Friday evening of our convention weekend. I had spent 13 hours at the venue dealing with vendor load in, and then headed downtown to an art show closing reception that I had organized for our creator guests. I got to the reception, popped off the top of a beer, and promptly got a phone call saying I needed to get home to take my wife to the hospital. Put the beer down, headed out, and hours later, Bram was part of our family. I came back to work on Sunday (lol). To this day, I have returning vendors ask me how my son is doing.

James Bialkowski

James Bialkowski is the mastermind behind the London Comic Book Convention and Shock Stock, both of which are held in London, Ontario, Canada. Both shows are successful, but in the last couple of years Shock Stock has gained the reputation of the place to be for its party atmosphere, great guests, and anything goes convention rules. Like its predecessor, Cinema Wasteland, the show is held in the same hotel where the guests stay, making it a self-contained weekend party. It was recommended to the authors of this book by Dyanne Thorne, so what else do you need to know?

James is a lifelong fan of pop culture, although his favorite media changes from time to time. He is probably best known for his incredible inventory of movies ranging from well-known mainstream hits to Italian zombie movies to European cult classics. James has an incredible amount of respect for film as an art form, and very little respect for the copyright laws that apply to film, as you will learn from his interview, along with a wide variety of convention stories, and his experiences with a Swedish movie star's beaver. Pictures of James and his close personal friends are below.

Can you give us a quick list of the fan conventions you have organized or attended?
Shock Stock is a labor of love. When I started organizing it, it was the first Canadian horror convention that wasn't piggybacking on a comic book convention or part of another convention. It's for the more knowledgeable horror fan. I had been on the convention radar for a while as a vendor so I had met a lot of people that could help me.

I had been to lots of conventions, including Cinema Wasteland and Chiller Theatre, as a vendor of bootleg DVDs: mainly European stuff that was never released here. I wanted Shock Stock to be like Cinema Wasteland, all contained in one hotel where all the guests and attendees would stay so everyone would be together all the time. I had a hotel all set up, but then they saw some of the promotional material for the show. Dyanne Thorne was one of the guests, and the hotel didn't like the images from *Ilsa, She Wolf of the SS*, so I had to scramble and found a hall downtown and we used it for the first 8 years. Now we're all in one building.

I also organize the London Comic Con, which is here in London, Ontario too. I went to the first Astronomicon in Michigan recently and it was great.

What is the strangest thing you have seen asked to be autographed?
In the past it was breasts, but now everyone wants selfies, or to take pictures of the celebrities with their phones. It was kind of funny to see people just hand their kids to William Shatner, who ended up holding them very awkwardly so they could take a picture of their kids with Shatner.

What is the most inappropriate thing a fan has done or said at one of your conventions? What about by a celebrity guest?
I had to go buy condoms for an adult film star who was a guest so they could have sex with a fan. Sometimes the fans ask very personal or awkward questions at the Q and A's and everything just stops.

What about the flipside? What is the sweetest or most touching thing a fan has said or done at one of your shows?

People have met and started relationships at my shows. I would love to host a wedding at one of my shows for two people who had met through one.

You interact with fans not only through your conventions but as a vendor of horror films and memorabilia. What is the strangest thing a fan has tried to sell you or request from you?

Vendors are big on trading. Lots of them will bring me the crafts they have made or home-made tee-shirts or movies they have made and want to trade for my stuff. For instance, in the case of the guy who wants James to buy 20 copies of his movie, sight unseen. One guy I do business with twice a year at Cinema Wasteland sends me all kinds of links to weird Russian videos, and he has me make him DVDs of them, but they have to be put in the exact order that he tells me or he won't watch them. I see the videos as I am editing, but I don't understand any of them.

Horror films include several sub-genres, like classic Universal films, slasher movies, dead teen-ager movies, drive-in schlock, etc. How do fans of different sub-genres interact with each other? Have you seen any funny or shocking confrontations between fans over the years?

There is an assumption that all horror fans have black fingernails, dyed black hair, and listen to nothing but Goth music. There is some of that, but when I'm booking music for my shows, it's rock and roll and metal. Some other shows will have nothing but Juggalo music by Insane Clown Posse. I'd rather have everyone all together rather than dividing them up into little groups.

When I was at the Calgary comic book convention, a 400 pound guy stepped on my foot and I yelled out "Jesus Christ!" A cosplayer dressed as Jesus Christ (at least I think it was a cosplayer) promptly appeared and offered to heal me. What is your personal WTF story from any convention?

Shock Stock has a reputation as a party show because it is located right in the middle of the bar district in London. Tony Todd, the actor from *Candyman*, was gone for two hours past his lunch, and he was taking advantage of our location. Nobody had any idea where he was, and he was going to be late for his segment. Someone in the green room said we should just say his name 5 times, and he'd appear, because that was the whole gimmick in *Candyman*. I said his name, and right on cue with the fifth one, the door flew open and in he came.

I've had Jesus at my shows too. Sometimes he does his makeup so he has blood coming from his crown of thorns, and he carries a water bottle so he can keep the "blood" wet. I think his real name is James.

What experiences have you had with fans who know far more about the themes of your various conventions than you would expect them to know? How do you deal with that situation?

There are lots of people like that. Some are completely wrong about what they think they know, but it is best to let them be and not correct them. Sometimes at Q and A's there are one or two really inappropriate questions about details from movies. I got into a really silly argument once about *Godzilla* movies, like which one was the first one in color and stupid little details like that.

What is your average convention attendee like, and which person really surprised you by being a fan?

For Shock Stock, 60 to 80% of the attendees are from out of town. We can't crack the local market.

For London Comic Con, it's the opposite. It's almost all local people. There might be everyone from the cashier at my grocery store to a bunch of soccer moms if someone like Norman Reedus is a guest. Geek culture is a lot more mainstream now.

The cosplayers are different from regular attendees. There are lots at the Comicon and hardly any at Shock Stock, maybe one guy dressed like Freddy Kruger or something. Horror fans are like that. If you go to Cinema Wasteland, maybe one out of fifty is in costume. Cosplayers walk around and socialize, but usually don't buy anything. Some of them are almost like celebrities themselves. If a costume is really great, I sometimes let the person in for free. We try to police the shows ourselves so we have a cosplay-safe environment.

What about haters? Have people come to your conventions just to say how much they hate horror or your particular guests?

I get a lot of that through social media, but not at the actual shows. When the guest list first comes out, there is a lot of chatter because people don't understand why I book certain guests like wrestlers. Popular wrestlers from the 80's and 90's really draw well. There are also a lot of stupid comments from people who won't read the website and find out answers to their questions that are right there in front of them. For the first four or five shows, I would get comments from a lot of people that they would come if my show wasn't so far away, and these were people who only lived an hour or two away in Toronto. In Toronto, it can take 90 minutes to go to the airport, so why not spend that time coming to the show? I got a lot of comments like that because I would book guests that they wouldn't bring into the Toronto shows.

What other celebrity encounters have you had at conventions? Feel free to tell us any funny, sexy and/or terrifying close encounters you have had.
One year I brought in the whole cast of the *Evil Dead* other than Bruce Campbell. I had to pick the one girl up at her sister's house in Michigan. I ended up in her sister's kitchen having coffee. Then we had to pick up the others, as well as Linnea Quigley. Everyone joked that as soon as we picked up Linnea we didn't have a chance of getting back across the border into Canada.

Another year I brought in the Italian progressive band Goblin. They do a lot of soundtracks. I had the composer and two of the original members, and had some Canadians to do the backline stuff. We were the first show to bring them in.

It is amazing to meet these people and have them end up in your room drinking tequila. I keep in touch with lots of them. I can go to Los Angeles now and stay with some of them. I've made some lifelong friendships.

Have you ever been mistaken for someone else at a convention, and thought "why the Hell did you think I was them?" Have you had any celebrity guests mistaken for other people?
Once, and it was hilarious. I was a vendor at Chiller Theatre, and I used to make so much money at that show that I would fly there. Normally I wear a horror tee-shirt, jeans and runners to these shows, but my wife had me dressed really nice that time. There were celebrities on the plane too, like Jerri Manthey from the second season of *Survivor*. When we got off the

plane, she went to get a ride or something and I ended up standing with a bunch of celebrities under the Chiller Theatre banner at the airport, so people were happily taking my picture too while Jerri was going "Who is that guy?" She wouldn't even take a cab with me.

People don't confuse celebrities with each other, but they can get confused on exactly what movies they have been in. That can cause some embarrassment.

What is the one that got away? Which celebrity were you this close to getting only to have them pull out at the last nano second?

Norman Reedus. It was the second year of the show. Everything had been confirmed. He had a high guarantee, but I was going to pay half, Sunrise Records was paying half, and Anchor Bay was contributing too. We were about to sign the contract. The whole inner circle of the convention knew about it. We were about to advertise when Fan Expo, who does the Toronto comic con, flexed its muscle and relied on a "no compete clause" to keep him from coming here. Now, I don't know if we could have done it, especially the extra security. We have good security, but not heavy security.

Kane Hodder had to cancel one year. We had advertised, but we had advance warning. He even did a video for our website announcing that he wasn't coming. People still showed up expecting to see him.

There are lots of people I contact every year, especially Europeans, not expecting them to come. I did get Christina Lindberg one year, from Sweden, and one guy paid her to autograph forty posters. I tried every year of the show to get adult star Christy Canyon, and she is finally coming. She was worried that she would have to sit around for three days, but I have it so she only has to be available for two days. We aren't an "adult's only" show, but 5 or 6 times I have brought in adult stars.

Cosplay has become an art form. What costume at any convention has totally blown you away and amazed you with its high quality and detail? What is the all-time worst costume you have seen?

I saw a tin man costume made of cornflake boxes. The best ones are those that replicate these Japanese cyborg characters. I don't know the characters because I don't follow anime or Japanese games, but the detail in the robot parts and guns is amazing. Sometimes the simple cosplays are just as good though, especially if you have people who are lookalikes for the actors.

What super fans have you encountered whose whole lives have been consumed with one topic or movie they live for?

There are lots of those guys. They are the ones who come for one actor and leave, like the one guy with his forty Christina Lindberg posters. I used to be able to pick trends when I was a video pirate. I could pick what foreign actresses had cult followings and guys would come in and pick up all 12 movies of one actress. I know one guy who buys a VHS tape of the movie *Street Trash* whenever he sees one. He's got them in Greek or whatever, and has about 40 of the American version. I used to do the same with different stuff to a certain extent. At first it was records, then it was 35 mm film, like Italian zombie movie trailers. I had a huge collection of that and then sold it, and now I collect records again. But, whatever I have been into has been horror or counter culture related.

How do celebrities react to their first conventions?

They don't know what to expect. They are often surprised that people still care and get humbled and shocked by the attention. I know a few who have never done shows who are too reluctant to try. First timers are a lot of fun.

How have fan conventions changed in your lifetime?

The major change is the cost. Originally, attendees would pay an admission fee and that would be it unless they bought something. There was no charge for autographs or pictures. The other big change has been the evolution of cosplay. It used to be that people would laugh at the guys who dressed up. Now people love to see the costumes. There are also now legitimate celebrities booked as guests.

Before you became a convention organizer you were a fan. Ever have any true fanboy moments encountering celebrities before you became one of their employers?

I met Bruce Campbell when I was in my early twenties. I had read about horror conventions in Fangoria. I took an eight hour bus trip to Chicago as a mini vacation to attend one. It was a real rock star thing. I got to hang with him.

Horror movies are an international phenomenon. Do you get many international fans at your shows?

Some guys came from England to the London Comic Con. There was a Finnish guy at Shock Stock one year. I was never clear if he came from Finland for the show or had just moved from Finland to Canada. I just know that he ended up in my hotel room making all these crazy Viking drinks.

Going back to Christina Lindberg, when she came over from Sweden, my daughters went to Build-a-bear and made her a stuffed beaver as a Canadian symbol, but then they dressed it in a leather jacket and an eye patch like she had in *Thriller*. I saw a documentary about her last year, and there she was with the same stuffed beaver in her living room on display.

Have you ever had a celebrity make strange demands on you in order to be a guest at one of your shows?

I back away from celebrities who have handlers. I don't want to pay extra so their coffee-getter can come with them. Some will demand that you account for every nickel and want to send someone to keep track of that. When you are dealing with booking agents, they want you to deal with everyone they handle. In order to get Shatner, I basically had to audition. I had to book three other guys through his booking agent to prove myself first. Sometimes you have to pay a guaranteed minimum to a celebrity, and you are responsible for that no matter how many tickets you sell. I try to avoid people with crazy high guarantees. There are a lot of people I would try to get before I'd pay to bring in someone like Brad Pitt.

OK, now it's all you: What is the one knock-'em-dead, blow-their-socks-off fan convention story that you haven't told us yet? It can be funny, sad, scary, sexy, heart-warming, terrifying, sexy, action packed, cerebral, sexy or gross. Did I mention it could be sexy?

The funniest involves these guys who made a movie called *Dear God No!* It was a throwback to the biker movies of the 1970's and was about a biker gang taking on Bigfoot. The guy who made it was a genius and created all these posters for it capturing the style of the time. I screened it at Shock Stock and it was great. I tried to bring up the two stars for the show but they look like Sasquatches themselves and were turned away at the border. So, I arranged for Cinema Wasteland in Ohio to show it. I was supposed to meet them there, and all I knew was that they were coming in a rented Dodge Charger. I kept an eye out for them but they were easy to spot because they had parked it across three parking spots. They were late because the show was in the same city they made *A CHRISTMAS STORY*, and they drove to the worst part of town to see the house it was shot at. Then, they tried to buy cocaine at the house across the street and ended up with guns drawn on them. They stayed in character for the whole show and were dressed in the colors of their fictional gang from the movie, the Impalers. Then, the host tried to start the movie early and they unplugged the projector. It was all a work, like in pro wrestling. They just did whatever they wanted. Wherever they went, there were beer cans everywhere.

THE SHOCK STOCK LINE OF STUFFED ANIMALS

THE CHRISTINA LINDBERG BEAVER

THE DYANNE THORNE SHE WOLF

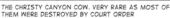

THE CHRISTY CANYON COW. VERY RARE AS MOST OF THEM WERE DESTROYED BY COURT ORDER

THE CHRISTY CANYON FOX, CREATED AFTER HER LAWYERS SUGGESTED THE COW TOY MIGHT NOT BE DIGNIFIED ENOUGH FOR THEIR CLIENT

Kevin Boyd

(Comics Relations Coordinator, Fan Expo HQ)

FAN EXPO HQ is the largest pop culture exhibitions group in Canada and one of the largest in the world. Collectively it hosts over 500,000 fans annually at FAN EXPO CANADA, FAN EXPO VANCOUVER, FAN EXPO REGINA, FAN EXPO DALLAS, TORONTO COMICON, DALLAS FAN DAYS, MEGACON TAMPA BAY, BOSTON COMIC CON and MEGACON ORLANDO.

They are industry leaders with respect to the number and quality of celebrities, creators, and cosplayers they regularly bring into their shows.

When Kevin Boyd kindly took time out of his schedule to answer our questions, he was in Dallas while simultaneously organizing shows in Dallas and Regina, Saskatchewan, two cities a mere 2300 kilometers apart.

If you are already a fan of fan conventions, you have probably already attended one of their shows. If you haven't, check out one close to you. They are professionally run and a lot of fun for the whole family.

A typical Canadian fan convention attendee.

Can you give us a quick list of the fan conventions you have organized or attended?
I organized my first comic show in 2002. From 2002-2007 I organized 9 events for Paradise Conventions. In 2007 I went to work for Hobbystar Marketing and worked on approximately 25 events for them, including Fan Expo Canada and the first Fan Expo Vancouver, but left in late 2012 after opening a retail shop, which I ran until 2015. I returned to work for Fan Expo HQ in fall 2015 and I've worked on over 20 events for them subsequently, including shows in Toronto, Vancouver, Regina, Orlando, Tampa Bay, Dallas and now Boston.

What is the strangest thing you have seen asked to be autographed?
A tattoo.

What is the most inappropriate thing a fan has done or said at one of your conventions? What about by a celebrity guest?
Everyone is awesome; I'd have a hard time thinking of something specific. I don't really work with the celebrities so I'm afraid I have nothing to share on that front.

What about the flip side? What is the sweetest or most touching thing a fan has said or done at one of your shows?
I've seen many people share stories about how Stan Lee changed their life in some way, and Stan rarely disappoints. He has a way of making you believe he's your best pal.

You interact with fans and vendors at conventions. What is the strangest thing someone has tried to sell at one of your shows?

Used clothing --- Like their old pants and shirts that no longer fit them. They had no collectible value whatsoever.

Your show features celebrities from different media and genres. How do fans of different sub-genres interact with each other? Have you seen any funny or shocking confrontations between fans over the years?

Generally people get along and are civil to one another. I'll hear from the back issue comics buying attendees about how they don't like cosplayers and they get in the way of their bin diving, but I've never seen an actual confrontation.

What experiences have you had with fans who know far more about the celebrities of your various conventions than the celebrities themselves? How do various stars deal with that?

I'm not really around the celebs much, but I do deal with comic fans who often know more about the characters and the issues done by the creator than the creators themselves. Most of them are great about it, and are impressed by the level of knowledge.

What is your average convention attendee like, and which person really surprised you by being a fan?

The average convention attendee is a renaissance person, a fountain of pop culture knowledge. Everyone is a fan of something, so I'm not really ever surprised. Fans come from all walks of life, and come in every shape and size.

What about haters? Have people come to your conventions just to say how much they hate pop culture or your particular guests?

I'm sure it happens, but they usually wait until they are safely back at home in front of their computer before they let their hate flow.

What other celebrity encounters have you had at conventions? Feel free to tell us any funny, sexy and/or terrifying close encounters you have had.

I'm so boring - I just look out for the comic book pros.

What is the one that got away? Which celebrity were you this close to getting only to have them pull out at the last nano second?

I almost had Stan Lee as a guest at one show, but he had to cancel. But he's subsequently come out to many of our events.

Cosplay has become an art form. What costume at any convention has totally blown you away and amazed you with its high quality and detail? What is the all-time worst costume you have seen?

I've seen some great massive, detailed costumes, like Hulkbuster Iron Man, or Groot. But every show there are amazing costumes, the amount of detail and love they put into these costumes is amazing. The worst, a guy in a paper bag dressed as laundry day Spider-Man.

What super fans have you encountered whose whole lives have been consumed with one topic or movie they live for?

I've encountered many, most memorably fans of the 1960's *Batman* show, or *Star Trek*.

What about stars who aren't convention regulars or are appearing at their first show? Are they surprised by how strong their fandom is? How do they react to their first conventions?

I'm sure the first one is an eye opener for someone not used to them.

Comic book conventions have gone from small gatherings to huge multimedia showcases. How has your show in particular changed and how has the type of celebrity who appears at them changed?

Our shows are always growing, so yes, they've gone from being dealer rooms with long boxes of comics to giant rooms with a little bit of everything as well as dealers with long boxes of comics. We see a lot more celebrities actively working on television shows and movies at events these days, they used to be people whose shows had been cancelled.

Before you became a convention organizer you were a fan. Ever have any true fanboy moments encountering celebrities before you became one of their employers?

I'm still star struck by certain comic creators, for instance we had Frank Miller at some of our events last year.

Photo ops are a convention favorite. Tell us about the more memorable ones you have seen.

I've seen celebrities get right into the moment with their photo, making faces and having fun with it.

Do you get many international fans at your shows, or fans of foreign pop culture?

We get lots of international fans at our shows. Comics, movies and television are popular all over the world and translated into many languages so it's not unusual to encounter someone who has travelled a long distance to meet a certain guest.

What would your dream guest be in the future?

Steve Ditko or John Byrne.

Have you ever had a celebrity make strange demands on you in order to be a guest at one of your shows?

No, mostly I get "please tell your boss I would love to be a guest."

OK, now it's all you: What is the one knock-'em-dead, blow-their-socks-off fan convention story that you haven't told us yet? It can be funny, sad, scary, sexy, heart-warming, terrifying, sexy, action packed, cerebral, sexy or gross. Did I mention it could be sexy?

Sitting in the office at a show and behind me is Stan Lee having a sandwich, to the left Adam West is getting some money change, to the right on the other side of the room is Burt Ward shooting the breeze with a member of the staff, and in another part of the room William Shatner is looking at his phone. I'm a little in awe because all of my childhood heroes are assembled in one place. Then Burt says "it's time for our photo op with the Batmobile", Adam shouts "To the Batmobile, old chum!", to which Stan yells out "Excelsior!" Shatner chuckled. Nerd heaven.

What keeps you going, organizing multiple shows per year, year after year?

The people, the pay, the love of comics.

I have been to conventions where there is one vendor who seems badly out of place, like they didn't know what kind of show they were buying a table at. Have you had any experiences like that?

On occasion, you'll see a vendor that doesn't fit. But sometimes that works, thinking outside of the box can reap rewards... or fail miserably

Ted Bohus

Ted Bohus is an accomplished horror film producer, horror magazine publisher and horror film historian. In short, he is just plain scary.

His most acclaimed film is *Deadly Spawn,* but he has directed, produced and acted in many others. His film *Nightbeast* gained fame through IMDb when it was confirmed as the first film credit of some guy named J.J. Abrams, who has done one or two things since then.

As a magazine publisher, he produces SPFX, Monster Bash, Monster Biz, Monster Mania, Monsterpalooza and others.

As an author, he has produced two volumes of *Candid Monsters,* collections of behind-the-scenes photos from classic movies.

Ted is also a convention veteran and can be seen most regularly at the Chiller Theatre shows, which are held twice a year. Check him and this great show out.

Can you give us a quick list of the fan conventions you have appeared at, as both a fan and celebrity guest?
No, not a quick list. There have been hundreds and hundreds. I have been at every Chiller Theatre ever, twice a year. There's Creation Convention, Monster Bash, Monster Mania, Fan X, Wonder Fest, Horror Find, lots more.

What is the strangest thing you have been asked to autograph?
Someone's naked ass. At least it was a female fan.

What is the most inappropriate thing a fan has done or said to you?
A guy came up and he had a problem with the blood and guts in my movies and said they were inappropriate for children. I told him to quickly go out and destroy all of the copies of Grimm's Fairy Tales and the Bible before a kid could see any of them.

What about the flipside? What is the sweetest or most touching thing a fan has said or done for you?
People bring me strange things they have found related to my movies, like Japanese posters or fliers for *Deadly Spawn,* as presents. Lots of times I

didn't even know they existed. And, this is authentic stuff, not bootlegs. I do a pretty good job on getting rid of bootleg merchandisers. Usually it just takes a letter.

Have you had people come up to you dressed as one of your characters?
Not really, but people come and show me their gigantic *Deadly Spawn* tattoos, ones that cover their entire arm or most of their back, or they show me pictures of their tattoos. I find some of them to be a little strange. Those are gruesome looking monsters.

When I was at the Calgary comic book convention, a 400 pound guy stepped on my foot and I yelled out "Jesus Christ!" A cosplayer dressed as Jesus Christ (at least I think it was a cosplayer) promptly appeared and offered to heal me. What is your personal WTF story from any convention?
Oh yeah, I've got a Jesus story. It was a show in East Rutherford and there was a guy drinking in the lobby of the Sheraton. He wrapped a tablecloth around himself and he looked exactly like Jesus. A bunch of us quickly gathered around him and struck a pose so we could recreate the painting *The Last Supper*. It looks just like it. Friends of mine have turned the picture into coasters and mouse pads. Maybe I'll make a poster of it someday. There's a copy of it in my new book *Candid Monsters*.

What experiences have you had with fans who know far more about you and your films than you could expect them to know? How do you deal with that situation?
There are lots of fans who are really invested in something. To them, the films they love are almost real. I enjoy meeting people like that but I don't always have time for what they want. They want to stand there and talk to you for an hour but maybe I need a half hour break to eat and go to the bathroom. Sometimes they'll just keep talking while I do that. When you're involved in films and publishing, you meet people like that.

What other celebrity encounters have you had at conventions? Feel free to tell us any funny, sexy and/or terrifying close encounters you have had.

Oh, I've had millions of celebrity encounters since I started going to shows in the 60's. Most of the people you meet are very nice. Gary

Busey was horrifying. He was nice to his fans, but treated all of the convention staff horribly. Monstrous. Linda Hamilton is great. One time she just sat and chatted with me for half an hour. Ali McGraw was very sweet. I had her autograph Robert Evans' book, *The Kid Stays in the Picture* because she was married to him and is mentioned in it. She said she'd take the book to get him to sign it, but I said it would be enough if she just gave me his address to send to him. Not only did she do that, but she told him about me and that the book was coming. Very nice lady.

Have you ever been mistaken for someone else at a convention, and thought "why the Hell did you think I was them?"
Liam Neeson. The older I get, the more often people think I'm Liam Neeson. I never understood why until someone showed me a recent black and white photo of him in a newspaper and I thought, "Ah crap. I do look like Liam Neeson."

Cosplay has become an art form. What costume at any convention has totally blown you away and amazed you with its high quality and detail? What is the all-time worst costume you have seen?
I've seen thousands of costumes and I have thousands of pictures of great one. My favorites are ones that recreate specific episodes of the original *Twilight Zone*. I saw a great one based on the *Eye of the Beholder* episode. The worst one ever was a guy who was supposed to be a human from the future world of *Planet of the Apes*. He just smeared some brown stuff all over his body, looked dishevelled and wore a loincloth. A very, very small loincloth. It was disgusting.

You have been photographed thousands of times. What is your favorite photo with a fan, and what was the one request that made you shake your head, laugh or throw up a little in your mouth?
Oh, there have been thousands of good ones. I'll send you some copies. There haven't been too many bad ones. Sometimes when someone has a gross or disgusting costume and they want a picture you just kind of smile and hope it is over quick. Nobody ever tries to pick me up or anything like you see a lot in shows. I'm 6'3" and weigh about 240 so I don't have to worry about that at least.

Gender bender cosplay continues to get more and more popular. Have you seen much of that at conventions? What was that like?

I don't pay attention to stuff like that. I'd rather look at the really great re-creations of old Universal Monsters or the crazy stuff some of the girls think of.

Before you became a celebrity you were a fan. Ever have any true fanboy moments encountering celebrities before you became one?

Not really. The only people who could have ever reduced me to the stupid fanboy level were the Beatles. Otherwise, I'm not a fan of anything in that sense.

Have you been interviewed and done panels at conventions? What are the funniest, strangest and most thought provoking questions you have encountered?

Oh, I've done hundreds of panels. Whenever any convention wants to do a B-movie panel they quickly call me and Fred Olen Ray. Sometimes the fans try to read too much into stuff, like claiming that *Deadly Spawn* is a metaphor for everyday life in New Jersey. It's just a horror movie, people!

Have you done any foreign conventions yet? What was that like?

No. I am cursed. I have been invited to shows in England, Canada and Japan, but every time I am busy doing a movie or something. The invitations only come when it is absolutely impossible to go. I would love to go to a show in Japan sometime. Their fans are amazing. Lots of times Japanese fans will come up to me in the States and ask when *Deadly Spawn 4* is coming out. There wasn't even a *Deadly Spawn 2* or *3!* But in Japan, they love trilogies, so distributors labelled my movie *Metamorphosis* as *Deadly Spawn 2* and *Regenerated Man* as *Deadly Spawn 3*. They aren't actually a series so for years I had no idea what they were talking about.

You are constantly on the road. What is the hardest part about travel, and your funniest story from being on the road?

I can't tell you my funniest stories. I can't tell anyone my funniest stories. The only part of one story I can tell you is about when I and Kevin Clement from Chiller Theater and Dave Baumuller from Horror Biz used to go together in a van to all of these shows together. One time Kevin was driving and he was cracking himself up as he told us this joke about 4 ducks. After several minutes of him laughing, he got to the punch line, and Dave and I looked at each other and said, "That makes no sense." Kevin thought for a second and said, "Did I say ducks? I meant skunks." Dave and I started laughing so hard then that we almost forced Kevin into an accident.

OK, now it's all you: What is the one knock-'em-dead, blow-their-socks-off fan convention story that you haven't told us yet? It can be funny, sad, scary, sexy, heart-warming, terrifying, sexy, action packed, cerebral, sexy or gross. Did I mention it could be sexy? I'm trying to sell some books here.

Oh, I hear you. I write books too. One time I was doing a show in New York, and the writer Harlan Ellison was there. He is a very short guy and at the time he was very egotistical. He was not liked at all in certain circles. Anyway, before our panel, a fan wanted a picture with me and Harlan and Harlan was very rude, and I figured I had to do something about that and shove a pen right through his balloon. When the time came for the panel, Harlan didn't just want to come out from behind a curtain like the rest of us panelists. He wanted 2 doors in the back of the room to suddenly fly open and then he would walk by the whole crowd and make this grand entrance as the final guest being announced. So they announce his name, and the doors fly open, and I look around and say "Where is he?" as he is coming down the aisle and walking to the podium. I got a big laugh from the crowd and a really ugly scowl from him.

One other time for Chiller Theater I was trying to get all of the actors who played the kids in the original *Willy Wonku* movie together for a reunion. Nobody had ever done that before, and most of them never acted after that movie. Peter Ostrum, in particular, who played Charlie, never acted again and had never done a personal appearance. He was working as a vet by this time. He had no interest in doing our show. I asked him what he really wanted and he said he needed an X-ray machine for his practice. I asked how much that cost and he said $10,000. I told him to come, and if he didn't make that much money in the 3 day show, I'd pay the difference. By Saturday afternoon he told me he already had his machine paid for. Now he does a few shows.

Anyway, it was the first time anyone had done a reunion of these kids, so I did a story on it too for my magazine, SPFX. Then, *The Rosie O'Donnell Show* called, and Rosie wanted them on her show too. I was supposed to go down with them and then Rosie was going to give a copy of my magazine to everyone in the audience. It would have been great, but at the last second the owners of the movie's music wouldn't let her use any of it, and she's really into movie themes and stuff, so she cancelled the whole thing!

TOP WAYS TED BOHUS HAS RUINED ENTRIES OF HARLAN ELLISON INTO COMIC PANELS
HEY! WHO LOCKED THIS?
Panel Room A1
WHO PUT SUPERGLUE ON THE TOILET SEAT?

#1 SIGN THAT SOMEONE WANTS TO TALK TO TED BOHUS AND NOT WITH HIM

Casey Cantu

(Director of ZiCon Anime Convention in Edinburg, Texas)

Can you give us a quick list of the fan conventions you have organized or attended?

Well I've attended many, mostly in the state of Texas but one all the way over in Japan. A-Kon, RealmsCon, South Texas Collectors Expo, San Japan, Ikkicon, RTX to name the ones here in Texas and Anime Japan in, well, Japan. That one was CRAZY HUGE! It was almost unbelievable the number of attendees and events they had there. I personally have helped with and organized a con called Omnicon for the past several years, South Texas Comic Con, and South Texas Horror Con. Now I'm running my own show ZiCon.

What is the strangest thing you have seen asked to be autographed?

Though I never saw it with my own eyes, a guest we had once told me he was requested to sign a baby. I don't quite understand why a person would want to do that to their child, and why they would waste an autograph! Are they never planning on washing that child's head? Ridiculous.

What is the most inappropriate thing a fan has done or said at one of your conventions? What about by a celebrity guest?

One fan wanted a guest of ours to record a message saying a very lewd remark (something along the lines of rape) and I quickly shut them down and explained to them why such a request was absurd. Then on another show we had a guest, who was asked to make a phone call to an attend-ee's friend, tell the person on the phone that "everyone was making babies down here." That probably was one of the craziest things I've heard a guest say.

What about the flipside? What is the sweetest or most touching thing a fan has said or done at one of your shows?

You frequently hear attendees say nice things to guests, so it's a bit hard to recollect any of them, but personally to me, a man brought his two young daughters over to me after opening ceremonies at my event and told me thank you for everything I do to make these shows happen, and the kids proceeded to hug me. It was a very touching moment.

You interact with fans and vendors at conventions. What is the strangest thing someone has tried to sell at one of your shows?

We usually screen our vendors beforehand, so nothing strange usually gets to hit the shelves. There are some vendors that will sneak in some bootleg stuff after they set up, and some are so blatantly bootleg its surprising they even thought someone would mistakenly purchase them believing to be authentic.

Your show features celebrities from different media and genres. How do fans of different sub-genres interact with each other? Have you seen any funny or shocking confrontations between fans over the years?

Surprisingly enough, everyone gets along rather well. Everyone who attends these conventions is all there for the same reason, to show love to their respective fandoms and let their geek flags fly. So, there is a mutual respect; of course, you'll have some who will pretend to have beef for the sake of it, but in the end, they take pictures together and just go about their way; it's always a good experience.

When I was at the Calgary comic book convention, a 400 pound guy stepped on my foot and I yelled out "Jesus Christ!" A cosplayer dressed as Jesus Christ (at least I think it was a cosplayer) promptly appeared and offered to heal me. What is your personal WTF story from any convention?

That's pretty hilarious! A pretty cool moment at one of the shows I had been working with was this one time, where a large guy was dressed as Snorlax decided to, as his character would, lay down in the middle of one of our major hallways during the event. Now we could have gotten angry and told him to leave or remove him, but one of my partners got out his phone, searched up the PokéFlute and played the sound. The guy promptly got up and moved out of the way as Snorlax does in the Pokémon games. It's always awesome to see people be in character.

What experiences have you had with fans who know far more about the celebrities of your various conventions than the celebrities themselves? How do various stars deal with that?

I have yet to experience that. There are some who know a lot about them, but usually what is very publicly known, so I haven't really seen a guest taken back by how much someone knows about them.

What is your average convention attendee like, and which person really surprised you by being a fan?

We have a very good mixture of die-hards and casual, so the average convention attendee for our shows is pretty much everyone. Your waiter at Olive Garden to a car salesman to a doctor. I've seen them all there and I've seen them all in cosplay. The community in the areas of which I work at or attend just seem to really love conventions and being part of that culture.

What about haters? Have people come to your conventions just to say how much they hate pop culture or your particular guests?

It's strange to say that people will spend their money and time, to attend something they don't enjoy, just to bash it. But it does happen from time to time. I've read reviews on our social media sites saying they thought the show was trash or boring, and that the guests we brought were nobodies, but it usually stems from them not understanding the event they're even attending. One year we had brought several actors from the *Power Rangers* series, and had a lot of complaints about our show and it "straying from what we usually do". Yet that show in particular is a show that celebrates Japanese arts, and the *Super Sentai* (or as we know them in the US, *Power Rangers*) are a big part of that, but still they were just salty that we didn't bring anime voice actors that year.

What other celebrity encounters have you had at conventions? Feel free to tell us any funny, sexy and/or terrifying close encounters you have had.

We once had a guest who was constantly jonesing for cocaine and kept asking his handler to go and score some for him. Now this guy was a huge dude and being a junkie who needed a fix was a pretty scary issue to deal with. He eventually went off on his own and found some, thankfully after he was off the clock. How he found a dealer in an area where he has never been to before is beyond me.

Have you ever been mistaken for someone else at a convention, and thought "why the Hell did you think I was them?" Have you had any celebrity guests mistaken for other people?

This has happened twice to me. The first, I sat at a booth of one of our guests who needed to go to the restroom. This guy approached the table and begin to tell me how "what I do is so undervalued and that he appreciates my line of work" and so on. It took me a little while but I quickly realized that he thought I was the guest, who mind you was 20 years my senior, bald, and outweighed me by about 40 pounds. I played along and told him that "it was fans like him that made it all worthwhile." I then proceeded to autograph a flyer for him and took a picture with him. All the while the actual guest was standing behind him, laughing the whole time. Another time I was, once again, sitting at a guest table, with the guest sitting next to me, and this attendee asked him if he was the guest and he said, "Nah, it's this guy" and pointed to me. The guy then approached me to ask me questions about the show, *The Walking Dead*, which the guest was a part of. I'm a Hispanic, the guest was African American, and we even had a banner hanging behind the table of the guest, and this guy still didn't get that I wasn't the guest.

What is the one that got away? Which celebrity were you this close to getting only to have them pull out at the last nano second?

I once lost 4 at once, but it wasn't the fault of the guest. The venue where I was trying to host the event was terrible, and they were extremely difficult to work with, thus forcing me to cancel the event. I had already booked 4 amazing guests that I had been wanting to see for years, only to have them slip through my fingers thanks to this ridiculous venue management.

Cosplay has become an art form. What costume at any convention has totally blown you away and amazed you with its high quality and detail? What is the all-time worst costume you have seen?

That's a very tough question to answer. The events I have gone to have had a plethora of incredible talent with people who clearly put a lot of time and effort into their craft. One cosplay that does linger in my mind, though, was this one woman in-particular dressed up as La Muerte from the movie *Book of Life*. Her make-up was incredible and the flame lights she had on her costume were awesome. As far as worse... I once saw a Godzilla made of spray-painted cardboard boxes, which was cool in its own way, but ... yeah.

What super fans have you encountered whose whole lives have been consumed with one topic or movie they live for?

Star Wars is an easy answer. There's this one cat who regularly shows up dressed as Count Dooku, every year, to every event. His car has "Count Dooku" license plates, he seems to carry around his gear at all times just in case someone asks him to bust it out. It's clear this is his life.

What about stars who aren't convention regulars or are appearing at their first show? Are they surprised by how strong their fandom is? How do they react to their first conventions?

Oh yeah, there have been some times where we will bring a star who hasn't particularly done anything in a while, and have a die-hard audience and an incredible reception. They get all choked up and will always leave our events feeling incredible.

Comic book conventions have gone from small gatherings to huge multimedia showcases. How has your show in particular changed and how has the type of celebrity who appears at them changed?

All the shows I have previously worked at have grown year after year, though the type of celebrities we bring haven't really changed. On the other hand, it has come to a point where the general public has become more aware of the media of which our guests are from, and have now begun to actively seek them out. So that's pretty cool.

Before you became a convention organizer you were a fan. Ever have any true fanboy moments encountering celebrities before you became one of their employers?

Surprisingly no, I quickly realized that celebrities are more receptive to you when you act like they're also humans instead of some god. So, I've always kept my chill despite being in the presence of people I've been a huge fan for. One instance I took a service elevator at an event I was promoting at, and a guest that I had been wanting to see for years was in the same elevator with me, I went crazy on the inside, but remained calm and collected on the outside.

Photo ops are a convention favorite. Tell us about the more memorable ones you have seen.

Unfortunately, I don't have a cool story about photo ops, they are usually rather smooth and nothing crazy really happens.

Do you get many international fans at your shows, or fans of foreign pop culture?

Living really close to the Mexican border we get a lot of attendees from across the way. It's cool to see how much of our media has penetrated theirs. So, they show up despite not really knowing the language to meet our guests, and it's always cool to see that interaction.

Panels are a mainstay of conventions. Have you ever had one get out of hand? What happened? Which celebrities knew how to shut down hecklers?

John DiMaggio, that man both knows how to make a panel get out of hand, and quickly wrangle it right back in. He has such an incredible presence, he had everyone there just hanging on his every word.

Do fans ever confuse the actor with the characters they portray?

All the time! We have people who will show up and are scared to talk to a certain guest because they think they'll be mean like they are in a particular show, but they turn out to be the biggest sweethearts.

What would your dream guest be in the future?

There are so many I can't even begin to state them, but as for most people, Stan Lee would be an incredible catch. I don't know how much longer he has, but hopefully my show will get large enough, quick enough, to eventually book him.

Have you ever had a celebrity make strange demands on you in order to be a guest at one of your shows?
No thankfully, other than food allergies and things of that sort. Usually, the strange requests come afterwards…

OK, now it's all you: What is the one knock-'em-dead, blow-their-socks-off fan convention story that you haven't told us yet? It can be funny, sad,, scary, sexy, heart-warming, terrifying, sexy, action packed, cerebral, sexy or gross. Did I mention it could be sexy?
I've pretty much told any sort of crazy stuff, except for this one time we busted our musical guest doing lines of coke in the green room before their show, but we really couldn't do anything, because they were just about to go on. But other than that, we do what we can to run a tight ship and keep our shows as family friendly as possible. So, we haven't really had any major issues thankfully.

What keeps you going, organizing multiple shows per year, year after year?
The fans, the attendees are awesome and despite a few bad apples, I love entertaining them. I'm an entertainer at heart, so to be able to do so like this is an exhilarating experience.

I have been to conventions where there is one vendor who seems badly out of place, like they didn't know what kind of show they were buying a table at. Have you had any experiences like that?
No, the vendors that we get usually are seasoned vets, though in our artist alleys we will have a couple of them. But our teams are usually very good at helping them get their footing, we even offer some of our volunteers to help at their table if they're feeling overwhelmed.

Cosplay Butterfly

Cosplay Butterfly a.k.a. Jesse from Toronto is often referred to as Canada's most beautiful cosplayer. One of her most famous prints as one of her signature characters, She Ra, is on the following page, so you can make up your own mind about that. I met her at the Saskatoon Entertainment Expo, and one of her many adoring social media followers announced loudly from fifty feet away that he recognized her butt and that he was going to bring his wife to meet her as she was also a big fan, so some people have obviously made up their mind on that point already.

She is also a very fun-loving person who was more than happy to pose for countless selfies, give advice about cosplaying and costume making, and tell some hilarious stories about her adventures as a cosplayer, displaying a very self-deprecating sense of humor. For the love of God people: don't just gawk at her, talk to her!

Unless of course you see her on a plane you are about to board. Then you should quickly sell your plane ticket to someone you don't like and hitch a ride with a biker gang to whatever your destination is. It will be safer.

Can you give us a quick list of the fan conventions you have appeared at, as both a fan and celebrity guest?
I have only ever gone to conventions as a cosplayer. The way I got into it was that when I was 13, I moved from Ottawa to Toronto. My best friend was going to Anime North, which is the big Anime show in Toronto, and we were reuniting at the show. Her mom was a professional theatrical

costume maker and she made both of us these amazing costumes. I was hooked. Since then, I've been to lots of shows all over Canada. In terms of American shows, I've been to Supertoy, American, Blizcon, and others. I've been to the New York Comicon once and would love to go back. It was such a huge show that I didn't get to see all of it.

What is the strangest thing you have been asked to autograph?
People's arms.

What is the most inappropriate thing a fan has done or said to you?
It was at a show that was attached to a convention centre that hosted a lot of business conferences. He wasn't even a fan. He was some businessman attending some conference, but he saw me and ran up to me, so excited. He offered to buy the pantyhose I was wearing for $100. For the record, I said no.

What about the flipside? What is the sweetest or most touching thing a fan has said or done for you?
There is no one example. There are dozens. My fans are great. Mexican fans in particular are so warm and friendly. They bring me candy, food, fan art, and lots of other things. One of them did my Cosplay Butterfly logo inside a piece glass using wires embedded in the glass. When it lights up, it is beautiful. Someone else made me a customized Hot Wheels car with my logo on it.

When I was at the Calgary comic book convention, a 400 pound guy stepped on my foot and I yelled out "Jesus Christ!" A cosplayer dressed as Jesus Christ (at least I think it was a cosplayer) promptly appeared and offered to heal me. What is your personal WTF story from any convention?
A fan dressed as a character from *Legend of Zelda* was playing the ocarina in front of my table at a show. They started playing the theme from *Jurassic Park*. Two cosplayers doing Sam Neill and Laura Dern came over, followed by two playing the leads from *Jurassic World*, and then half a dozen people wearing those inflatable dinosaur suits. None of them had known each other before the show and this hadn't been planned, and they improvised a dance number. I had my own private dinosaur party. I love it when things like that happen.

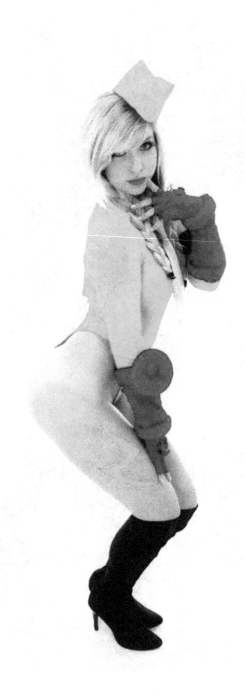

Have you ever been mistaken for someone else at a convention, and thought "why the Hell did you think I was them?"

Never. Heck, I'm still surprised when people recognize me as me!

You have been photographed thousands of times. What is your favorite photo with a fan, and what was the one request that made you shake your head, laugh or throw up a little in your mouth?

Sometimes a male fan will put his hand around me lower than he should. I just grab it and move it to where it should be.

You have been interviewed and done panels at conventions. What are the funniest, strangest and most thought provoking questions you have encountered?

The strangest and funniest are the marriage proposals. Who thinks that is going to work? My least favorite is: "How did you become cosfamous?", which is cosplayer slang for "how did you become a successful cosplayer?" People are so disappointed when there is no guidebook or secret formula for them. It is a matter of luck and timing.

You are constantly on the road. What is the hardest part about travel, and your funniest story from being on the road?

The hardest part was almost dying. I was doing a show in Mexico, and they had brought the guests down a couple of days early to give us all a big tour of the Xilapa vicinity. One of the stops was a beautiful coffee plantation. There was this roadside ice cream stand, and everyone said you had to try this homemade ice cream. It was good, but I ended up with some kid of intestinal infection, and I am sure it was from that ice cream. It was horrifying because as soon as I came home, I ended up spending four days in a hospital near death surrounded by people who couldn't tell me what was going to happen or what exactly I had.

Now it's all you: What is the one knock-'em-dead, blow-their-socks-off fan convention story that you haven't told us yet? It can be funny, sad, scary, sexy, heart-warming, terrifying, sexy, action packed, cerebral, sexy or gross. Did I mention it could be sexy? I'm trying to sell some books here.

The first time I did a show in Mexico, I was again brought in early with the other guests. We were given a big tour of the area, saw an incredible museum and one of the other stops was the pyramids. We climbed up the biggest one and watched the most beautiful sunset. It was just mesmerizing. I spent the next year yelling at my boyfriend about it, so when I was invited down to the show again, we decided to make it our vacation. I was given a free ticket by the show and he bought his own. We ended up on separate flights as a result of that. He flew out first, and when I went to get on the plane, I was told that my passport was invalid because there was water damage on it. I ran over to customs and was told it should be usable, but if the airline was refusing it, all I could do was go to the passport office and get one on an expedited basis. I went there as soon as it opened the next day, and showed them my I.D. I don't have a driver's license, so I had to use my health card. It was expired, so I ran over to the health card office, and that was a hassle because I didn't have a passport or driver's license to use as I.D. I finally got the health card and ran back to the passport office. You need someone to sign for you as well who is over 18, and I had my sister with me. She was refused because her I.D. was invalid too. I started calling everyone I've ever met in my life to find someone who could come down immediately to the passport office, and my stepfather was able to come just before the office closed. Everything was ready to go and the passport printer promptly crashed, and it couldn't be printed on any other printer because that was the only special printer that could do passports that they had. So, I had to go back the next day. I went directly to the airport, and promptly sat there doing absolutely nothing for two hours because the plane was delayed. We got on the plane and sat in it for another two hours before we were told they had to switch us to another plane. That took another 3 hours. That was the worst three days of my life. No matter what I did the gods were not with me.

Have you done any foreign conventions yet?
Several in Mexico. My first one off the North American continent will be a show in Honolulu.

Alexander Craddock

Can you give us a quick list of the fan conventions you have organized or attended?

Primarily METROCON, which I've owned since 2009 with my partner. We did an offshoot convention in the Fall of 2013 called Asylum, but it didn't take off, so we only did it once. I've probably been to over 100 conventions in the past ten years or so, big and small.

What is the strangest thing you have seen someone ask to have autographed?

So personally, I have a dollar bill that I carry in my wallet and get celebrities to sign it whenever I meet them. Whenever it fills up, I get a new dollar and the other one goes into my stash of memorabilia. I've also seen somebody ask to have their baby signed - that was weird.

What is the most inappropriate thing a fan has done or said at one of your conventions? What about a celebrity guest?
We had a fan stalking one of our female voice actor guests. We ended up having to give her a greatly increased security detail for the weekend. That was probably the worst. As far as a guest, we had a band at our convention once that got so angry at me it almost turned physical. When it didn't, they eventually went back to their hotel room and trashed the place. I guess they forgot they had a credit card on file for damages, so they ended up having to pay for broken chairs, holes in the walls, etc.

What about the flipside? What is the sweetest or most touching thing a fan has said or done at one of your shows?
I have had a number of fans say that whether directly or indirectly, METROCON changed their life. I had one fan who explained he was suicidal until he went to METROCON and realized he wasn't alone, and that was probably a decade ago. We're still friends, and he started going to conventions all over the place. He's married now - he met his wife at a convention.

You interact with fans and vendors at conventions. What is the strangest thing someone has tried to sell at one of your shows?
We had a vendor a few years back who snuck in by lying about what they were selling - they were ACTUALLY running a gambling game where you'd pay money for spins on a rigged wheel of some kind, and you'd always get "just close" and think spending $5 might win you that prize. It was awful, we had them escorted out by the police. We frequently have to stop vendors from selling things like tasers or weapons - they think it fits in with the cosplay weapons or airsoft replicas they're already selling, and we have to remind them we don't want to ACTUALLY arm people.

Your show features voice actors, cosplayers, live action actors of both recent and vintage shows, and comic book creators. How do fans of different subgenres interact with each other? Have you seen any funny or shocking confrontations between fans over the years?

Actually, just this past year - there was an older couple not even attending our event, just staying at the hotel by chance, who were huge *Doctor Who* fans back in the sixties. They wandered over, never having heard of anime (our show's primary focus) and had an absolute blast. They became solidly adopted as grandparents by a small group of younger cosplayers who gave them the whole "experience" and grand tour. It was very touching, and the older couple emailed me after the show to talk about how awesome it was for them!

When I was at the Calgary comic book convention, a 400-pound guy stepped on my foot and I yelled out "Jesus Christ!" A cosplayer dressed as Jesus Christ (at least I think it was a cosplayer) promptly appeared and offered to heal me. What is your personal WTF story from any convention?

I can't think of one offhand, but I can almost bet you it was a Deadpool - those people are everywhere.

What experiences have you had with fans who know far more about the celebrities of your various conventions than the celebrities themselves? How do various stars deal with that?

Since we deal mostly in anime, we don't get a lot of crazy rabid fans, but there were definitely a few moments with Scott McNeil where he had to lean over to his liaison and fact-check something. When a career is long and full of so many different things, it can be hard to keep track of it all!

What is your average convention attendee like, and which person really surprised you by being a fan?

Our average attendees are teenagers and young adults, like at most anime conventions. We also get a lot of families, since we're one of the only events that is STRICTLY PG-13, with no adult material at all. I'm usually surprised by the extremely conservative types, or the ones I know personally from other walks of life - one of the city council members brings his daughter every year and they dress up in cosplay and have a blast.

What about haters? Have people come to your conventions just to say how much they hate pop culture or your particular guests?

Sure, absolutely. We also typically have religious protestors outside of our venue talking about how anime will make you go to hell, etc.

What other celebrity encounters have you had at conventions? Feel free to tell us any funny, sexy and/or terrifying close encounters you have had.

I got to drink a beer with Danny Trejo and hang out with Gary Busey in his pajamas once, that was pretty cool. Peter Mayhew bummed a cigarette off of me and we chatted about *Star Wars*. I have a bad habit of not realizing people are celebrities until the next day...

Who is the one that got away? Which celebrity were you this close to getting only to have them pull out at the last nanosecond?

We had Monkey Punch slated back in 2005-ish and it didn't work out due to a family emergency. He was the guy who created *Lupin III*, so he's a huge figure in anime. We ended up booking him the following year, though, so I guess he didn't REALLY get away!

Cosplay has become an art form. What costume at any convention has totally blown you away and amazed you with its high quality and detail? What is the all-time worst costume you have seen?

I love seeing weird stuff that surpasses costume and becomes almost an art installation. There was a mermaid being pulled around on a wagon this past year that I loved - she had the wagon all dressed up like a rocky outcropping. The worst costumes I see are actually banned at our event - they're what I call "shock costumes" and I despise them. If you're working a costume just to purposefully be a dick, or to get a rise out of somebody or spread hate, go home. Trolls should stay on the internet.

What about stars who aren't convention regulars or are appearing at their first show? Are they surprised by how strong their fandom is? How do they react to their first conventions?

First-time convention celebrities are one of my favorite groups. They are almost universally humble = and have no idea how much their work means to people.

Comic book conventions have gone from small gatherings to huge multi-media showcases. How has your show in particular changed and how has the type of celebrity who appears at them changed?

We get a lot more casual attendees, people just swinging through for the day. It's also a lot easier to tell people what I do now.

Before you became a convention organizer you were a fan. Ever have any true fanboy moments encountering celebrities before you became one of their employers?

Absolutely - I am a huge *Spartacus* fan, and I got to bring Manu Bennett out to one of our Fall shows. It was amazing. I had missed him at other conventions several times before, and always kicked myself for it, but I loved having him there.

Photo ops are a convention favorite. Tell us about the more memorable ones you have seen.

I love the candid selfies. When folks are just casually interacting and genuine with each other and the celebrities - I also love celebrities who don't mind doing that with fans they see in elevators or hallways. Not that I don't understand why they charge for photo ops formally, but the ones who know their fans are the reason they get to do what they love.

Do you get many international fans at your shows, or fans of foreign pop culture?

For sure - we have several regulars who come from Europe.

Panels are a mainstay of conventions. Have you ever had one get out of hand? What happened? Which celebrities knew how to shut down hecklers?

Like I said, we're a strictly family friendly show, so we really shut stuff down if it starts to get too... er... adult. Some of those *Voltron* panels get out of hand.

Who would be your dream guest in the future?

Hayao Miyazaki. Hands down. If you've never read anything about him or watched the documentary on Studio Ghibli that's out, I highly recommend it. He's the Walt Disney of anime - he completely revolutionized animated storytelling and remains possibly the most humble and exacting person in the industry

Have you ever had a celebrity make strange demands on you in order to be a guest at one of your shows?

Oh sure - I had a celebrity just recently request to be on the highest possible floor because they wanted a quiet room, but the same rider asked to be on the closest possible floor to the convention levels because they don't like elevators. I've also had a band request a cheese platter in each room, their dressing room, the green room, and on each side of the stage. That was weird.

OK, now it's all you: What is the one knock-'em-dead, blow-their-socks-off fan convention story that you haven't told us yet? It can be funny, sad, scary, sexy, heart-warming, terrifying, sexy, action packed, cerebral, sexy or gross. Did I mention it could be sexy?

I actually can't think of one... I'm sure I've got a million but now I'm on the spot! It's hard because ALL of my stories since I took over the business usually involve conventions in some wa]y. I met my wife doing conventions and performing, my daughter goes to them now, all of my friends are at least nearby to the geek scene and convention world, if not directly involved in it.

What keeps you going, organizing shows year after year?

Easy - it's the way I can provide the most happiness for the most people, year over year. Even if it impacts people in the tiniest way, it still is putting out happiness into the universe, which we can always use more of.

Dave Dyer

In 2009, the Webster Groves native and Webster University alumnus opened an entertainment-based company, Dyer Straits Productions (DSP). He and his business partner, Susan Koerkenmeier, developed

CON-TAMINATION, a yearly horror and pop culture convention, the only one of its kind in the St. Louis area.

Can you give us a quick list of the fan conventions you have organized or attended?

I started off in 1999 as a vendor selling out of print toys at conventions in Chicago, Nashville, and all over the Midwest. I started my own show, Con-tamination, 6 years ago. It's produced by Dyer Straits Productions, which consists of me and my wife. We do everything.

What is the strangest thing you have seen asked to be autographed?

A prosthetic limb signed by Peter Mayhew, who played Chewbacca in the *Star Wars* movies. Other than that, just the standard boobs and butts.

What is the most inappropriate thing a fan has done or said at one of your conventions?

The word fan is derived from the word fanatic, so by definition fans are fanatics, and some fans become stalkers. I was at the Resinhead show back in the 90's, and security finally had to kick a guy out for harassing one of the stars, and he kept finding ways to break back into the hotel. It was scary.

What about the flipside? What is the sweetest or most touching thing a fan has said or done at one of your shows?

It was something that happened to me at the Monster Weekend show. Dee Wallace was there, and I gave her a postcard of her late husband, Chris Stone, from the Christmas movie *Santa Claus*, and it had a stamp of his signature. She broke down crying. She is absolutely adorable.

You interact with fans and vendors at conventions. What is the strangest thing someone has tried to sell at one of your shows?

I am very good friends with adult film legend Seka, and she helps me get adult film stars for my show. I rely on her to keep track of them and what they are doing because I run a family show and I have very strict rules. One year, Kitten Natividad was here, and she wouldn't play by the most impor-tant rule, which is to keep the naughty bits covered up. I ended up yelling at Seka because Kitten was selling photos with her boobs hanging out, and she wouldn't stop doing it.

Another year I had a guy selling body parts. They weren't real, but they looked like real flesh and you could put them on your keychain or whatever. They looked like something out of *The Texas Chainsaw Massacre.*

Your show features celebrities from different media and genres. How do fans of different sub-genres interact with each other? Have you seen any funny or shocking confrontations between fans over the years?

Nothing shocking. After all, they are all among like-minded fans. *Star Trek* fans aren't going to fight *Star Wars* fans, and Michael Myers fans aren't going to fight Jason Voorhees fans.

When I was at the Calgary comic book convention, a 400 pound guy stepped on my foot and I yelled out "Jesus Christ!" A cosplayer dressed as Jesus Christ (at least I think it was a cosplayer) promptly appeared and offered to heal me. What is your personal WTF story from any convention?

It was something that happened at my show this year. This guy had made his own Punkinhead costume, and it was incredible. He won the cosplay contest. He had built a pump of some kind into one of the arms of his costume, and he would put his hand over people's mouths and shoot alcohol into their mouths.

What experiences have you had with fans who know far more about the celebrities of your various conventions than the celebrities themselves? How do various stars deal with that?

I wouldn't say it is common, but it is not uncommon for fans to outdo celebrities, especially anything *Star Trek* related. This year I had Debra Shillen, you played the Yellow Ranger in *Time Force*, and she was blown away by the fans who just eat and drink that show and anything Power Ranger related.

What is your average convention attendee like, and which person really surprised you by being a fan?

They aren't rude, but they are socially awkward. They work a 9 to 5 job and don't get out much. It's the same at all of these shows, because they get to come to these shows and be among kindred spirits and feel normal. They're great.

What about haters? Have people come to your conventions just to say how much they hate pop culture or your particular guests?

It has always existed but now it has gone too far because of social media so you can be a hater and not pay any money to do it. Every year there are people bashing my show on Facebook, but it happens to everyone, even big shows like HorrorHound and Flashback. There is no show that doesn't get at least some of it. All you can do is turn the other cheek and move on, but what I really hate is that there are some shows that encourage their fans to bash other shows.

What other celebrity encounters have you had at conventions? Feel free to tell us any funny, sexy and/or terrifying close encounters you have had.

Oh I have lots of stories, mainly from the '80's and mainly from bars. I've drank with Kane Hodder, Ken Kirzinger, even Gary Clark from *Day of the Dead*. My favorite story is probably when at the hotel where the show was being held, I heard this beautiful music, and I walked around a corner and there was porn star Ron Jeremy sitting at a baby grand piano playing a concerto, and it was amazing. He's actually quite the Renaissance man. He has 2 or 3 degrees but prefers to make his living doing porn.

Have you ever been mistaken for someone else at a convention, and thought "why the Hell did you think I was them?" Have you had any celebrity guests mistaken for other people?

Not lately. Back in the '80's it was Jon Bon Jovi.

What is the one that got away? Which celebrity were you this close to getting only to have them pull out at the last nano second?

This happens every flipping year. I had a *Halloween* reunion booked with George Wilbur, Carmen Filipi and Sasha Jensen, and I was left with only Wilbur. Having only one person kicks the reunion idea out the door.

Cosplay has become an art form. What costume at any convention has totally blown you away and amazed you with its high quality and detail? What is the all-time worst costume you have seen?

The all-time best was Punkinhead this year, but there was also a great Babadook, as well as some great *Silent Hill* nurses. Also Barf, John Candy's character from *Spaceballs*. Someone did a good job on that one. The worst one was this lady dressed as a kitty cat. She looked like an extra in a bad low budget porno.

What super fans have you encountered whose whole lives have been consumed with one topic or movie they live for?

Besides *Power Rangers*, *Star Trek* and *Star Wars*, I have met a Freddy Krueger one, *Ghost Busters*, including one with a proton pack that looked functional. There are lots of anime fans, but I'm not into that so I don't know the characters.

What about stars who aren't convention regulars or are appearing at their first show? Are they surprised by how strong their fandom is? How do they react to their first conventions?

We just had one of those. Glenn Ennis did all of the stunts in *Freddy vs. Jason*, Collossus in *Deadpool* and more recently played the bear in *The Revenant*. We popped his convention cherry, so to speak. We went out of our way to make him feel at home, and he loved it. He had a great time. We ended up going for cocktails with him on Sunday night, and we're good friends now.

Fan conventions have gone from small gatherings to huge multi-media showcases. How has your show in particular changed and how has the type of celebrity who appears at them changed?

I have gone out of my way to not change my show. 1500-2000 fans and 9 celebrities is perfect. I want to keep it intimate. I don't like big shows. What's the point of having 30 celebrities if the guests can't see half of them?

Before you became a convention organizer you were a fan. Ever have any true fanboy moments encountering celebrities before you became one of their employers?

It was back in the 90's at the Hollywood Collector shows. It was produced by Ray Court, who became a mentor to me. He was a master of booking old school celebs. At one show he had both Lois Lanes, Noel Neill and Margot Kidder. I told Noel that I loved her character so much that my daughter's middle name is Lane. She was a really petite lady, maybe 5 foot 3, and when she started to tear up, so did I. It was amazing.

I did a great *Battlestar Galactica* reunion with most of the original TV cast. Richard Hatch was there and didn't let on to anyone that he was sick, and he was dead 3 months later, so the memories of that are now very special too.

Photo ops are a convention favorite. Tell us about the more memorable ones you have seen.

I hate photo ops. It is price gouging at its worst. Why should you stand in line for hours so you can spend $300 for a photo with Stan Lee? It's crazy! You're ushered in like cattle and then shooed away as quick as possible. Why not just have the stars at the table, and if they want to let you take a photo, fine? I never offer them, and the only one I have paid for is one with Alice Cooper.

Ken Deep

Ken Deep is commander in chief of L.I. Who, which is the abbreviation for the Long Island Dr. Who convention. It is often run in conjunction with another convention, L.I. Geek., which has to be the best name for a science fiction and fantasy convention ever. It has featured such guests as Greg Berger, Wendy Padbury, Paul Mc Gann and Bruce Boxleitner. It also holds the record for the weirdest venue. Read on and discover why.

Can you give us a quick list of the fan conventions you have organized or attended?
Attended, no. There are hundreds. Organised: L.I. Who, L.I. Geek, L.I. Quest

What is the strangest thing you have seen asked to be autographed?
A missile. A model of a missile, but a missile.

What is the most inappropriate thing a fan has done or said at one of your conventions?
To a female celeb "You look older."

What about the flipside? What is the sweetest or most touching thing a fan has said or done at one of your shows?
Several. A young terminally ill lady crying while her heroes were hugging her and showering her *with love.*

You interact with fans and vendors at conventions. What is the strangest thing someone has tried to sell at one of your shows?

Doctor Who sex toys.

Your show features celebrities from different media and genres. How do fans of different sub-genres interact with each other? Have you seen any funny or shocking confrontations between fans over the years?

Luckily no. I have seen strange reactions from other hotel attendees to our costumed attendees.

When I was at the Calgary comic book convention, a 400 pound guy stepped on my foot and I yelled out "Jesus Christ!" A cosplayer dressed as Jesus Christ (at least I think it was a cosplayer) promptly appeared and offered to heal me. What is your personal WTF story from any convention?

When our venue cancelled on us only two weeks before the event, the local airport stepped up and offered to host the convention. We held a sci-fi con while arriving passengers passed through the vendor area.

What experiences have you had with fans who know far more about the celebrities of your various conventions than the celebrities themselves? How do various stars deal with that?

They're pretty good with handling strange questions. Often the celebs like to correct misinformation that circulates in fandom.

What is your average convention attendee like, and which person really surprised you by being a fan?

They're smart and worldly. Informed and well read.

What about haters? Have people come to your conventions just to say how much they hate pop culture or your particular guests?

No, that wouldn't be welcomed. We run positive events.

What other celebrity encounters have you had at conventions? Feel free to tell us any funny, sexy and/or terrifying close encounters you have had.

When I was much younger, I had the chance to meet some of the *Doctor Who* actors that aren't with us anymore. Meeting my heroes had an impact on me then, but as time passes it has more significance to me. I cherish those memories.

What is the one that got away? Which celebrity were you this close to getting only to have them pull out at the last nano second?
The wonderful Richard Hatch from *Battlestar Galactica* passed away two months before we were scheduled to have him. That was crushing because we were looking forward to having him join us.

Cosplay has become an art form. What costume at any convention has totally blown you away and amazed you with its high quality and detail? What is the all-time worst costume you have seen?
I've seen some incredible costumes over the last decade. It seems like the skill level has increased over the last ten-fifteen years. Some of the *Aliens* cosplayers and the *Doctor Who* cosplayers always amaze me.

What super fans have you encountered whose whole lives have been consumed with one topic or movie they live for?
We have a young lady who idolises Carrie Fisher. She looks like her, dresses like her. It's incredible how influenced she is by her.

What about stars who aren't convention regulars or are appearing at their first show? Are they surprised by how strong their fandom is? How do they react to their first conventions? They usually admit they enjoyed it more than they expected. One first timer was amazed by how loving the fans were and what a sense of community there is.

Fan conventions have gone from small gatherings to huge multi-media showcases. How has your show in particular changed and how has the type of celebrity who appears at them changed?
The cost of high-end talent has skyrocketed. It makes the stars less accessible to fans and fan conventions.

Before you became a convention organizer you were a fan. Ever have any true fanboy moments encountering celebrities before you became one of their employers?

Yes, when I was 15 I met Jon Pertwee, the Third Doctor from *Doctor Who*. He was larger than life, funny and charismatic. It was electrifying. I knew I wanted to run a convention after that. It only took 27 years.

Photo ops are a convention favorite. Tell us about the more memorable ones you have seen. Doctor Who stars with lightsabers, I love the cosplayers who dress like the character that the actor portrays.

Do you get many international fans at your shows, or fans of foreign pop culture?
Yes. L.I. Who is an international event. It humbles me to think a fan from Australia flies nearly 24 hours to be with us.

Panels are a mainstay of conventions. Have you ever had one get out of hand? What happened? Which celebrities knew how to shut down hecklers?
Yes. Game shows can get out of hand. I've never really seen someone heckle a guest.

Do fans ever confuse the actor with the characters they portray?
Only with the questions they ask. "Why did you flip the _____ switch in episode __?"

What would your dream guest be in the future?
I'd like to see celebs embrace the fan run conventions more.

Have you ever had a celebrity make strange demands on you in order to be a guest at one of your shows?
Yes. A live chicken was the weirdest!

OK, now it's all you: What is the one knock-'em-dead, blow-their-socks-off fan convention story that you haven't told us yet? It can be funny, sad, scary, sexy, heart-warming, terrifying, sexy, action packed, cerebral, sexy or gross. Did I mention it could be sexy?
I enjoy the quiet, private conversations that take place on car rides or in the green room. Little discussions about life that humanise the guest.

What keeps you going, organizing multiple shows per year, year after year?

The attendees and volunteers enjoying themselves. They don't always know that I'm watching, but I can see it in their eyes.

I have been to conventions where there is one vendor who seems badly out of place, like they didn't know what kind of show they were buying a table at. Have you had any experiences like that?

No. Everything goes over the last decade.

THE GOOD THING ABOUT HAVING A CONVENTION IN AN AIRPORT IS THAT WE CAN GREET THE GUEST OF HONOR AS SOON AS HE ARRIVES.

L.I.. WHO- THE WRONG PLACE TO ASK IF THERE IS A DOCTOR IN THE HOUSE.

#1 RULE AFTER PROVIDING CELEBRITY GUEST WITH A LIVE CHICKEN: DON'T ASK.

Danielle DeNicola

If you want to spend a few minutes pleasantly on the internet watching something other than cat videos, do a google image search of Danielle Denicola. You will be amazed by the wide variety displayed in her dozens of different costumes, which she makes herself. She also writes, paints, is an avid gamer, and can make anything from armor to weaponry. She is also a professional model, and some beautiful prints of her are available online. But, a picture is worth a thousand words, so check out several thousand words worth of her.

Can you give us a quick list of the fan conventions you have appeared at, as both a fan and celebrity guest?

I've appeared at quite a few! My favorites to attend as a fan are Blizzcon, Colossalcon, and Katsucon. I've been a guest at CollectiveCon, Tampa Bay Comic Con, Comic Con Revolution, Ocala Comic Con, Treasure Coast Comic Con, Space Coast Comic Con, and many others.

What is the strangest thing you have been asked to autograph?

An arm! And a shirt... I think that's as strange as it gets.

What is the most inappropriate thing a fan has done or said to you?

Online is a battleground, so I think the top tier is probably the unsolicited dick pic.

What about the flipside? What is the sweetest or most touching thing a fan has said or done for you?

Messages about inspiring others to cosplay are the sweetest moments for me. I had a very apprehensive start and needed that push to start doing it, so being that for others is a good feeling.

Have you had people come up to you dressed as one of your characters (i.e. one you are also cosplaying)? Does it get competitive or is it all just part of the fun?

Yes! Attendees, fans, and friends have all cosplayed the same thing as I have, and it's definitely all part of the fun. A friend actually cosplayed the same thing I did on the same day who was staying in the same hotel room and we shared a prop all day for photos. I don't think it should be a competition.

When I was at the Calgary comic book convention, a 400-pound guy stepped on my foot and I yelled out "Jesus Christ!" A cosplayer dressed as Jesus Christ (at least I think it was a cosplayer) promptly appeared and offered to heal me. What is your personal WTF story from any convention?

LOL. That's an incredible story. Mine has to be this year at Katsucon, when I started hearing loud shouts, whipped my head around, and saw 20 men dressed as old women (complete with canes, wigs, glasses, outfits, etc.) yelling various renditions of "get off my lawn," "you young whippersnappers," *and other 'old people' tropes. I was so confused, yet so amused.*

You are a model, cosplayer, gamer and streamer. Are people surprised you are so talented? Do they expect you to be one thing but not the others?

Sometimes people are impressed with all the different hats, but oftentimes I find that we are online 'entertainers' and any way we can entertain is accepted—be that Twitch, cosplay, You Tube, or anything else. I think more people are surprised I have a full-time job outside of cosplay than anything else.

What experiences have you had with fans who know far more about you than you could expect them to know? How do you deal with that situation?

I haven't really had an encounter like that as of yet... but with Twitch and the internet in general, I don't think I would be terribly surprised.

What other celebrity encounters have you had at conventions? Feel free to tell us any funny, sexy and/or terrifying close encounters you have had.

Christy Carlson Romano came up to me when I was dressed as *Kim Possible* and asked to take a photo with me, which was right when I started, and I was STOKED. She even posted it on her Facebook page.

Have you ever been mistaken for someone else at a convention, and thought "why the Hell did you think I was them?" It can be either mistaking you for someone else, mistaking your character for someone else, or both.

People confuse me and Danielle Beaulieu CONSTANTLY. I'm not sure why, because we're about almost a foot different in height, and don't really look alike. For some reason, though, since we have the same first name, people always confuse us in person. We joke about it. We actually have a pretty funny prank we're planning because of it, ha-ha.

Cosplay has become an art form. What costume at any convention has totally blown you away and amazed you with its high quality and detail? What is the all-time worst costume you have seen?

Crymson Cosplay's Fiddlesticks is what comes to mind first, because he just debuted it at Katsucon this year and it was INCREDIBLE. I see so many talented cosplays though, it's hard to pinpoint one.

The worst, on the other hand, was when 2 people made 'twin tower' costumes complete with fire at Dragon Con one year. Usually I wouldn't point out a 'bad' cosplay because it's supposed to be a fun hobby and people

putting others down for bad craftsmanship is just unnecessarily mean....
but this one was very tasteless. Some things shouldn't be joked about, you
know?

*You have been photographed thousands of times. What is your favorite photo
with a fan, and what was the one request that made you shake your head,
laugh or throw up a little in your mouth?*
I like the fun ideas, like a Harley Quinn cosplayer asked to take a photo
with me as Poison Ivy and then proceeded to drop to the floor while
the Joker she was with pointed his fake gun at me. It's all about having
fun!

*Gender bender cosplay continues to get more and more popular. Have you
met a male version of your character at conventions? What was that like?*
I LOVE genderbends. That's mainly all I did the first year I cosplayed.
There's an artistic freedom that is really fun to play around with, with just
enough guidelines to keep you on track. I love when I see different genders
at cons meet up, we usually take photos together.

*Before you became a celebrity you were a fan. Ever have any true fangirl
moments encountering celebrities before you became one?*
Absolutely! Before I made cosplays, I wrote for a game news website. I had
one viral article about Amazing League of Legends Cosplays and Missyeru
was one of the cosplayers featured. I ended up seeing her at Katsucon in
2016, before I knew anyone in the community, and rather than accept the
opportunity to talk to her, I got really nervous and walked in the opposite
direction. She has no idea to this day, and now I would consider her a
friend! One day I'll bring it up.

*Have you been interviewed and done panels at conventions? What are the fun-
niest, strangest and most thought-provoking questions you have encountered?*
I've done both, yes! Questions are usually all the same, asking about favorite cosplays, etc. The best question I can think of is when the Social Media
and Cosplay panel I was on completely derailed when someone asked us
about our favorite Pokémon and then it became a huge *Pokémon* discussion. It was super fun. However, I always enjoy the people asking how to
get into it. I mentioned before about needing a push to get started and I

always like to try and be that for others, because they don't know what they're missing!

Have you done any foreign conventions yet? What was that like?
Not yet, but I'm leaving the country this year for Canada!

You are constantly on the road. What is the hardest part about travel, and your funniest story from being on the road?
The hardest part about travel is never feeling 'settled.' Living out of a bag definitely wears on your psyche. My funniest story is every time I show up to a normal public location in an extravagant costume. It always confuses the general public so much.

OK, now it's all you: What is the one knock-'em-dead, blow-their-socks-off fan convention story that you haven't told us yet? It can be funny, sad, scary, sexy, heart-warming, terrifying, sexy, action packed, cerebral, sexy or gross. Did I mention it could be sexy?
Mine's scary! At Dragon Con one year I was walking through the glass tunnel between hotels and heard a crazy loud thud. Turns out one of the football fans for the big game that was also going on that weekend had decided to throw a chair off his hotel balcony. It hit a girl in the head but LUCKILY she was dressed as Loki and her horns literally saved her life. CRAZY!

You are a pro cosplayer, and a damn good one. What tips do you have for fans who aren't at your level?
Everyone starts somewhere! It's cliché, but it's true. Malcolm Gladwell said it takes 10,000 hours to be great at something and it's so true, just START and you're already on the right track!

WHEN COSPLAYERS DON'T HAVE TIME TO CHANGE AND PACK BEFORE FLYING TO THE NEXT CONVENTION.

Katie George

I first learned of Katie George while doing research for this book. Some of the convention organizers I spoke to listed her as one of the best (and often the best) cosplayer in North America when it comes to being able to actually portray the character she is dressed as. This should come as no surprise when a little bit of research online revealed that in 2014 she won a major cosplay competition in Japan for her performance as one of her characters. To put that in context, the country that invented cosplay and has the most cosplayers in the world named her as the best cosplayer in the world. She is that good.

Because of her incredibly busy schedule, the interview with Katie was done by email but I hope to meet her in person one day as she is obviously a fascinating person who has a lot of experience as a cosplayer and is intelligent, forthright, and doesn't take any crap (intended or unintended) from old fanboy interviewers who write books about fan conventions.

Can you give us a quick list of the fan conventions you have appeared at, as both a fan and celebrity guest?
I've been going to cons since 2004, ranging from a handful a year to maybe about 8-10/year so the only way to provide a "quick list" would be to mention the ones I always attend every year (because they're in Atlanta): MomoCon, DragonCon, and AWA.

What is the strangest thing you have been asked to autograph?
An arm.

What is the most inappropriate thing a fan has done or said to you?
Although it's definitely happened to me, I honestly have never been traumatized enough to remember any particular anecdote on the fly.

What about the flipside? What is the sweetest or most touching thing a fan has said or done for you?
I love it when fans in the past have gifted me with handmade items! Handwritten letters, artwork, baked goods, little knitted plushies... It's so meaningful and sweet to receive a gift that someone put their heart into.

Have you had people come up to you dressed as one of your characters (i.e. one you are also cosplaying)? Does it get competitive or is it all just part of the fun?

I love running into people wearing the same costume as me because it's fun to compare construction notes (or character love, if they didn't happen to make their own costume), and you instantly know they have great taste! Some people get really anxious when they see other cosplayers in the same outfit, because they might be worried the interaction could be negative (like a passive-aggressive diss or a dirty look), so if someone seems to be actively avoiding eye contact with me, I try to respect their wishes not to interact.

When I was at the Calgary comic book convention, a 400 pound guy stepped on my foot and I yelled out "Jesus Christ!" A cosplayer dressed as Jesus Christ (at least I think it was a cosplayer) promptly appeared and offered to heal me. What is your personal WTF story from any convention?

Every year, DragonCon falls on the same weekend as the Chick-fil-A bowl, so football fans used to wander into DragonCon before they started checking badges more actively. One year, a Clemson fan looked so much like Alan Tudyk (best known for Wash from *Firefly*) that he successfully went around convincing people he actually WAS him to cater... let's say, "positive attention" from women. His resemblance was so strong, had he been/ looked about 15-20 years older, he might have fooled me, too (Alan was in his 40s, this guy was probably 25-30). I sometimes wonder if he ever properly deceived some unsuspecting or intoxicated congoer...

You are a model, cosplayer, and entertainer. Are people surprised you are so talented? Do they expect you to be one thing but not the others?

I think most of my followers are interested in my work BECAUSE I make my own costumes (as opposed to how I look in them), so it's probably not much of a surprise that I can craft relatively well. But even after 15 years, I still glow with pride whenever strangers at cons are shocked or impressed that I make my own costumes (they probably don't know how long I've been doing it, though, so it's not as impressive as they might think, ha-ha!).

What experiences have you had with fans who know far more about you than you could expect them to know? How do you deal with that situation?

I absolutely love it when I run into someone who asks me a specific detail about my life or costume because they pay attention to my Instagram stories or actually read my (very long) post captions. The fact that they care enough to remember something small means a lot to me!

What other celebrity encounters have you had at conventions? Feel free to tell us any funny, sexy and/or terrifying close encounters you have had.

I once had Alessandro Juliani ask me to record some lines from *The Miracle Worker* because he wanted to capture an authentic Alabamian accent for a theatre production of the show he was directing. (I actually don't have an accent, but I can fake one perfectly because I grew up around them.) To thank me afterward, he took me out drinking with the cast of *Battlestar Galactica* who was at DragonCon that year (2009), and they all sang me Happy Birthday at midnight when they found out it was my birthday (September 7, so every few years, DragonCon falls on my birthday).

Have you ever been mistaken for someone else at a convention, and thought "why the Hell did you think I was them?" It can be either mistaking you for someone else, mistaking your character for someone else, or both.

I once had a mom with 3 young children FULL ON think I was Anne Hathaway and not just a cosplayer dressed as Selina Kyle. It was pretty adorable, and I was VERY flattered! I also get confused for other tall female cosplayers every once in a while, like my friend Amazon Mandy (which I also take as a compliment!).

Cosplay has become an art form. What costume at any convention has totally blown you away and amazed you with its high quality and detail? What is the all-time worst costume you have seen?

I loved meeting Josh Hart (J. Hart Design) at Katsucon this year, because he has definitely elevated the art of cosplay to new heights in a way that few have with his couture tailoring skills, exquisite material selection, and gorgeous embellishment work. ALL of his costumes are positively breathtaking, and he documents his builds on social media, which is a treat for a community that doesn't often get to see the "proper" way to construct couture garments. As for the worst costumes, I really dislike when people try to use cosplay to offend or troll others. It's not funny; it just makes you look like an asshole.

You have been photographed thousands of times. What is your favorite photo with a fan, and what was the one request that made you shake your head, laugh or throw up a little in your mouth?

I don't like when strangers ask for me to kiss them for photos, even if it's just on the cheek. It makes me really uncomfortable.

Before you became a celebrity you were a fan. Ever have any true fangirl moments encountering celebrities before you became one?

I would NEVER call myself a celebrity, like ever, so let's reword that question to "Before you became a cosplayer, you were a fan of other cosplayers you saw online?" I absolutely fangirled Lindze when I saw her at my first DragonCon in 2006, and now she is one of my best friends in the world. That happens with cosplayers more often than you think!

Have you been interviewed and done panels at conventions? What are the funniest, strangest and most thought provoking questions you have encountered?

I can't think of any specific examples, but I recommend watching Cosplay! Crafting a Secret Identity for a fantastic documentary on being a cosplayer. [https://www.pbs.org/video/cosplay-crafting-secret-identity-cosplay-crafting-secret-identity/]

Have you done any foreign conventions yet? What was that like?

I have! I've done 2 events in Japan, 3 in Mexico, 1 in Germany, and 1 in London. They are all VERY different. Japan's cosplay scene is very much about escapism from their rather strict social code, so you get the sense that cosplay events are very cathartic for them; Europe LOVES cosplay competitions, so that elevates the craftsmanship of their cosplay scene in a really awesome way; and Mexico has one of the most fervent fanbases I've ever seen. It is a BLAST to watch them passionately geek out over what they're into with infectious enthusiasm.

You are constantly on the road. What is the hardest part about travel, and your funniest story from being on the road?

I don't travel much anymore, but traveling with pre-styled wigs is such a pain. I used to just bring styling tools and products to the con, rather than travel with them in large, bulky box rigs. I'm glad I don't make armor costumes, because I couldn't imagine hauling those around to non-local cons without something arriving broken or in bad shape!

OK, now it's all you: What is the one knock-'em-dead, blow-their-socks-off fan convention story that you haven't told us yet? It can be funny, sad, scary, sexy, heart-warming, terrifying, sexy, action packed, cerebral, sexy or gross. Did I mention it could be sexy?

What sort of "sexy" stories are you hoping for? The question is creepily worded, dude.

You are a pro cosplayer, and a damn good one. What tips do you have for fans who aren't at your level?

Do your research! Personally, it's my favorite part of the process. Research techniques, materials, and the source itself. If you try to dive head first into your build without any research, your finished product will never look as good as someone who spent the first 1-3 months of their cosplay project planning out how they were going to tackle every element of the costume.

Todd Haberkorn

Todd Michael Haberkorn is an American voice actor and director who has provided voices for English-language versions of <u>anime</u>, films, and video games. While Haberkorn was working in theater, he joined <u>Funimation</u> as a voice actor, with minor roles in *One Piece*, *Black Cat*, and *Peach Girl*. Since then, he has voiced characters such as Natsu Dragneel in *Fairy Tail*, Italy in *Hetalia: Axis Powers*, Hikaru Hitachiin in *Ouran HighSchool Host Club*, Allen Walker in *D.Gray-man*, Death the Kid in *Soul Eater*, Tsukune Aono in *Rosario + Vampire*, Kimihiro Watanuki in *xxxHolic*, and Yamato Akitsuki in *Suzuka*. He has also worked in Los Angeles as an actor, director, producer and writer.

You are an incredibly prolific voice actor. Do fans ever come up to you imitating one of your own characters?

All the time! I take it as a compliment. Often, I hear fans that mention how I inspired them to pursue voice acting – and that's one of the greatest pieces of feedback one could ever receive. Truly.

You have appeared as Spock in fan productions of Star Trek. For some people, Star Trek isn't entertainment; it's a religion. Has anyone ever thought you were being disrespectful or blasphemous of the "true" Star Trek?

No. Luckily, *Star Trek Continues* has been seen as nothing but a respectful journey displaying love for the franchise and passion to make something of quality. Now if CBS would just get in touch with me about this next season…

You are one of the hardest working celebrities on the convention circuit in terms of the amount you travel and the number of shows you do. What response have you gotten in other countries? How do Japanese people react to your portrayal of Japanese characters?

The Japanese love my *Dragon Ball Z* work and *Sgt Frog* work for sure. That's always great to hear. Internationally – it's gotta be *Fairy Tail*. Fans love Natsu and I can't blame them. After 276 episodes, 2 movies, and now another season – there's a lot to watch!! The thing is - the love is the same. It may be in a different language or a different continent, but the admiration is the same. It's remarkable.

In anime, you have voiced characters in incredibly popular franchises with intensely loyal fans, like Black Butler and Fairy Tale. How do those fans compare to Trekkies?

It's interesting…the fandom passion is the same, but the vitriol and ownership is really only in the Trekkie world I've found. That's where a lot of negative energy can bubble up to the surface so quickly. Where Trekkies feel they should decide how a franchise should conduct future episodes or that they were owed something from a franchise. I don't see that hardly at all in the anime fandom. Again, both sides have a ton of love for their respective franchises – it's just a bit different on the Trek side.

Star Trek recently had its 50th anniversary. Did you take part in the celebrations at all?

I was working! Ha. Wish I could've been there, but my celebration was working on the last *Star Trek* movie – so, that's fun for me. But, it's amazing to see the franchise endure over the decades and continue to ignite fans new and old.

Your voice is a big part of your career. At conventions, do you ever get so hoarse that you have to call it a day to save your voice?

Absolutely. I am fortunate enough to work every day behind the mic. And yes, talking at a con all weekend can definitely hurt the pipes. So, I do have to be conscious of that and take care to be safe with my voice so I can do this till I'm 90. Fans are respectful when I mention I can't do their favorite attack line 'cause of work – so it's good!

Mitch Hallock

ComiCONN and CT Gamercon are both run by Mitch Hallock, a life-long Connecticut comic book fan who discovered gaming conventions through his sons. Besides bringing in great celebrity guests and veteran artists, Mitch has added an additional twist to ComiCONN by holding it in a casino. Not only is it a great venue, it allows him to stage Las Vegas-style revues as part of the show. Besides organizing conventions and collecting, Mitch is involved in every aspect of fandom, including podcasting. Read his great interview and learn how to become Harrison Ford`s BFF by taking a photo of your own retina, and how to get a famous comic book artist to call you a whore!

Some of the many friends of Mitch Hallock.

Can you give us a quick list of the fan conventions you have organized or appeared at, as both a fan and celebrity guest?

I organize two Connecticut conventions. ComiCONN is at the Foxwoods Casino every year, and I have organized CT Gamercon for the last 2 years. I used to take my sons, who are huge gaming fans, to the PAX (Penny Arcade Exhibition) East show every year, which is the biggest gaming convention in the world. We loved the displays, games and demos. I have gone to comic conventions my whole life.

What is the strangest thing you have seen someone ask to have autographed?
I had Lee Meriweather, Burt Ward and Adam West booked for the same show, and Adam West died literally two months before he was supposed to come. We turned the show into a celebration of his life. Fans came from all over the country. We actually sold more tickets after he died than before. One guy wanted to drive his full-sized Batmobile replica into the show to have it autographed, and I refused. I told him to take a part of it off, bring it in and have that autographed.

hat is the most inappropriate thing a fan has done or said at one of your conventions? What about a celebrity guest?
Nobody is ever disrespectful in person. They save that for the internet.

What about the flipside? What is the sweetest or most touching thing a fan has said or done at one of your shows?
Each show has its own stories. One year we had Dean Cain from *Lois & Clark*. He was doing photo ops, and a lady came up and she was not just trembling, she was shaking. She was totally speechless. He had to calm her down just so she could have her photo taken. I asked him if that was typical. I guess I've been around the show for years, so you get used to it and the fan aspect diminishes. It's kind of like being someone who makes sausages or hot dogs. Once you see what goes into them, you never eat them. But when I asked Cain, he said you have to talk to these people and calm them down. You don't know what went into their life. Maybe their parents fought, or they had a bad childhood. He said, "People could watch our show and forget all of their problems. We could solve any problem in an hour. It was very reassuring. During the five years *Lois & Clark* was on, people could come home and know that Superman would save the day. We inadvertently saved a lot of people that way. Sometimes we compelled people to become writers, artists, directors."

People like Sam Jones from *Flash Gordon* or John Wesley Shipp from *The Flash* or Kevin Conroy from *Batman* all have similar stories. TV actors never hear the laughter or the applause. But they can come to these shows, and it's like a curtain call for them. It's their chance to talk to the people who made them successful.

For me, it still brings up all kinds of memories. One time I was talking to Lou Ferrigno on the phone, and suddenly I remembered 1978 and being at Radio Shack with my dad and telling him we had to buy the new antennae and have it up by 8:00 because *The Incredible Hulk* was on that night. When your dad is passing the message on to the sales clerk, you never think that one day you'll be talking to the Hulk.

What is the strangest thing a vendor has tried to sell at your shows?
Nothing. All of my shows are PG-13. I personally check all displays before the shows open to make sure nothing inappropriate is for sale. You do hear about stuff, though. A couple of years ago there was a vendor at the Philadelphia Comicon selling sex toys. Years ago I heard of some shows where vendors sold human bones. I find that disgusting. It's not proper.

Your different shows appeal to different subgenres. How are the fans different?
Originally at the comic book show, all of the guests were comic book artists. Comic book fans would line up at 5 or 6 a.m. for a 10 o'clock opening. They all wanted to be the first in line to get something signed or to find the best deals. Now we have TV actors, voice actors, and movie actors. All of the fans are different. The first time I had a gaming show, nobody showed up for the opening of it, which I thought was weird because there were lots of pre-sales. But by 2 or 3 in the afternoon, the hall was full. Gamers will stay up all night playing games, go to bed at 5 or 6 in the morning, and get up at noon. They couldn't figure out why we wanted to shut at 11 p.m. They wanted to stay until 2 or 3 in the morning.

Video gamers are very calm, relaxed and laid back. Comic book fans are constantly running around, seeing what back issues different vendors have and who has the best prices. Cosplayers are a whole different animal entirely. They are there to socialize and not shop. How is a guy dressed like Spider-Man going to have a wallet?

When I was at the Calgary comic book convention, a 400 pound guy stepped on my foot and I yelled out "Jesus Christ!" A cosplayer dressed as Jesus Christ (at least I think it was a cosplayer) promptly appeared and offered to heal me. What is your personal WTF story from any convention?

It wasn't at my show, but I accidentally stood on someone's cape on an escalator. It didn't end well.

Another time, I was attending the New York Comicon, and I see this guy wearing a trench coat come down the escalator and go into the men's room. I didn't think anything of it until he came out of the men's room wearing nothing but a Batman cowl, cape and grey body paint. He didn't even have a utility belt. By the time he got to the top of the escalator he was arrested.

What experiences have you had with fans who know far more about the themes of your various conventions than you would expect them to know? How do you deal with that situation?

I thought I knew a lot until I ran a trivia contest at one of my shows. I've been reading comics since I was 4, but I couldn't believe the minutiae some people know. It's like when I was at my local comic book store after I saw the *Black Panther* movie. I thought I knew a lot about the character, but then a stranger turns around and gives me a complete oral history of the character. Sometimes people will follow me around the comic book store because they recognize me and want to give me a complete list of guests they want at my next show. I mean, I'm just there to shop. I've had people send me novel length emails full of suggestions. Some people are walking encyclopaedic databases. They will know every voice actor on every episode of a given anime show.

What is your average convention attendee like, and which person really surprised you by being a fan?

For the comicon, the average guest is a 30-year-old male with kids. The most surprising guests I've had were two nuns. I thought they were cosplayers, but they were two nuns who were comic book fans. They bought copies of the Pope John Paul II comic Marvel did in the '80s and the complete series of Billy Tucci's Jesus book.

What about haters? Have people come to your conventions just to say how much they hate horror or your particular guests?

No. Lots of writers and artists tell me that people will bash the Hell out of them on the internet and then come to a convention and politely ask for an autograph. There is a big difference between the internet and real life. I have had some artists tell me that they have had fans come up to them at shows and scream "Oh my God! You killed my favorite character!" and they have to explain that they are just trying to earn a paycheque, not destroy people's dreams. I've had almost the whole team behind the *"Death of Superman"* story as guests and they have all said that the DC office received death threats for that. But I get 20,000 people a year at my show, and no haters.

What other celebrity encounters have you had at conventions? Feel free to tell us any funny, sexy and/or terrifying close encounters you have had.

When I was a kid, I went to a convention in New Haven, Connecticut with a friend of mine. My friend asked, "Do you want to meet Wally Wood?" and I said, "Who the Hell is Wally Wood?" and my friend said, "The guy standing beside you." I looked and there was this old guy asking. "Don't you know who I am?" and I had to say no. Then I went home to read the copy of *Daredevil #7* I bought, and it was drawn by Wally Wood.

Two years ago, I brought in Kevin Smith. We were hosting an event called "An Evening with Kevin Smith" and it started at 7:30. His plane didn't arrive in New York until 4 and it is a two-and-a-half-hour drive. Anyway, he made it here by 6, but he wanted to shower and eat. I took him into the hotel and there was a crowd of people waiting for him. I had to do an imitation of a football player and tackle people to get him through. So after he had showered and eaten, I wanted to get him to the stage without having to fight through a crowd. The security team for the hotel took us to what they called the secret service elevator to bypass the lobby. We ended up in the bowels of the hotel. It looked like a horror movie with clouds of steam. Kevin Smith said he felt like a mafia guy being taken to be killed. Then we come across a chalk outline of a body on the floor. Kevin Smith and I just stopped dead and stared at it. The security guy said it was just a joke because Kevin wasn't the first guy to make that comment. Then he took us to another secret elevator, and we came up in the middle of the stage.

I got yelled at by Howard Chaykin once. I hated him for 20 years. I went to a show in 1991 and stood in line to meet him. I wanted to show him this comic I had written and drawn called *The Adventures of Mitch and Merle* about me and a friend of mine. I did a weekly strip for two years for a college paper until I got fired, then under a pseudonym for the same paper until they found out it was me, and then self-published. I had a little bit of fame and was a cult figure for two years. I sold tee-shirts and was on a local cable show. I asked him a lot of questions about how to get an agent and royalties. He asked me if I was trying to tell stories or make money. I said I wanted to make money. He yelled that if I only wanted to do comics for the love of money and not for the love of art, I was a whore and he didn't have time for whores. I asked him what his comics sold for and he said two dollars each, so I said he was a two-dollar whore. He screamed for me to get out in front of a crowd of people. It was embarrassing. In 2010, I had to interview him for a podcast, and I told him why I had hated him for so long. He couldn't believe I had wasted so much energy that way. He explained that he did a lot of drugs back then and had no memory of the incident. He has been a guest at my shows since then and still feels bad about it. Every year on his birthday I send him a message, HAPPY BIRTHDAY FROM YOUR FRIEND THE WHOREMASTER.

Have you ever been mistaken for someone else at a convention, and thought "why the Hell did you think I was them?" Have you had any celebrity guests mistaken for other people?

Jay Leno. I have a long chin and grey hair so for 30 years people have mistaken me for Jay Leno. I don't see it. One time I ended up in line at a store behind the real David Letterman and people thought he was going to turn around and beat me up.

Comic artists are often mistaken for other people. Fans don't know what the artists look like, so they rely on the little tent cards on every table. I had Keith Giffen and Kevin Maguire here when they were drawing for *Justice League*. Maguire had to go to the bathroom, and this kid came up with a stack of books for Maguire to sign. Giffen tried to explain that he wasn't the artist, but the kid didn't believe him. He's a bit of a wiseass, so he started signing Kevin Maguire's name to all of these comics. Maguire wasn't happy when he came back to the table.

Who is the one that got away? Which celebrity were you this close to getting only to have them pull out at the last nanosecond?

You mean other than Adam West? People told me that he died just so he wouldn't have to do my show. I already had posters and tee-shirts of him made. I had the very last footage taken of Adam West to advertise my show, and then I couldn't use the commercials.

Cosplay has become an art form. What costume at any convention has totally blown you away and amazed you with its high quality and detail? What is the all-time worst costume you have seen?

There is one guy who comes every year, Tom DePetrillo of Extreme Costumes in Rhode Island. He makes these 10-foot-tall costumes like Iron Man and Bumblebee from the *Transformers*. He was supposed to debut his Hulkbuster costume at my show, but the paint wasn't dry. When he debuted it at a different show, his video got millions of views. He can walk around in these suits and even pick stuff up with the robot arms.

The worst was a guy who walked around with a thimble on his finger and said he was Rumpelstiltskin. He was simultaneously lame and very creative. Another time an overweight guy came wearing Underoos. He tried to squeeze into a little boy's shirt and jockey shorts, and it wasn't pretty.

What super fans have you encountered whose whole lives have been consumed with one topic or movie they live for?

There are so many guys like that. There is one Batman cosplayer, Bob Desnomie, who does a perfect Adam West impression and has all the mannerisms down cold. He knows every stitch of his costume. He also impersonates Bobby Darin. His brother is a Sinatra impersonator. Bob is also a member of the 501st Legion and can play a Stormtrooper or Darth Vader.

My shows can be like a theatre production with lots of audience participation. John Wesley Shipp said they were like a church revival. I had an idea to do an Adam West tribute called the Dark Knight Club, with Bob coming out in a tuxedo but wearing the cowl and cape, and singing "Ain't That a Kick in the Head" as a Bill-Murray-type lounge singer, and the Joker as a stand-up comedian and Catwoman as a torch singer. Burt Ward and Lee Meriwether loved it. We did the stage up like the Batcave and ran it like one of the old Dean Martin Roasts on TV, with stills from the '66 Batman show being shown on a big screen in the background. Every year I have a different theme like a Broadway revue.

How do stars react to their first conventions?

They get really into it. The show is held in a casino, so they are surrounded by people having fun. We have celebrity poker games with people like Sean Dunn, comic book artists and fans. It's like walking into the bar in *Star Wars*. You might see Michael Colter having a drink or Jesse Quick from *The Flash*, Violett Beane, singing karaoke. Because we are in a casino and not just a convention hall, we can do many different things.

How have conventions changed over the years?
They are far more expensive. The first one I went to I paid a buck, and that was it. It used to be all the guests were artists, and maybe one celebrity from years ago like Soupy Sales. They were not a cool thing for actors to be involved in. Now conventions are big business, because you can bring in Sylvester Stallone and people will pay $400 for his autograph. You've got people like Sigourney Weaver and Richard Dreyfuss doing conventions, and you never used to see that. Big guarantees for celebrities have driven up prices. Some shows are celebrity-driven. My shows are comic book conventions, so you have to have some superhero connection. I don't go to a football game to watch baseball players.

I try to keep admission to my shows at $30 or less, kids ten and under free. Photo ops and autographs are $20 to $40. Vendors like it, because people aren't spending all of their money on one celebrity and everyone gets a piece of the pie.

Before you became a convention organizer you were a fan. Ever have any true fanboy moments encountering celebrities before you became one of their employers?
I interviewed to be an intern for the Dik Browne studio once. I was interviewed by Roy Doty, who used to draw the *Laugh-In* comic strip. He was in a bad mood. His daughter was there and read my stuff and was laughing out loud. He took one look at it and said I didn't know how to draw hands. He told me to spend five or six months drawing hands and then try again.

Mike Zeck used to go to the same comic book store as me. My mom told him to call me and try to talk me out of being a cartoonist. I was just thrilled that Mike Zeck called me.

Panels are a mainstay of conventions. What is your most memorable one?

I arranged to do a 40th anniversary panel for *Star Wars*. Roy Thomas agreed to take part and he wore his original *Star Wars* shirt from when the movie came out. This tee-shirt was part of a run of 13 with Ralph McQuarrie art and was only given to people like Mark Hamill and the producer. Roy is really fit and can still wear it. Howard Chaykin took part even though he hates *Star Wars*. He has refused to do *Star Wars* panels in San Diego and New York, because he says everyone else associated with it became a millionaire and he became a "hundred-aire". He said he only did my panel because he had called me a whore. I tried to get George Lippincott, who got the toy and comic book deal for *Star Wars* and who at the time lived nearby in New Hampshire, but he was extremely sick at the time, and didn't do shows anyway. On the day of the panel, it was just supposed to be Thomas and Chaykin, but there was this third guy hanging around that nobody knew. Lippincott decided to come on his own and did the whole one-hour panel. It was great. You can find videos of it online.

Who would be your dream guest in the future?
Harrison Ford, but he doesn't do shows. My dream would be to have him and Stan Lee in the same show. Then I could retire happy.

John Byrne would be a dream. I would love to have Steve Ditko. He's a recluse, but I found his address. I wrote him a letter inviting him to be a guest, and three days later I got a letter back saying he had no desire to talk about the past and there was no point discussing things that happened 30 to 50 years ago. I even went where he lived once. I don't recommend that. Some friends of mine went and one of them knocked on the door as a joke. We were taking a picture of us standing in front of the name plate saying S. DITKO when the door swung open and Ditko yelled, "What the hell do you guys want?" He slammed the door in our faces.

OK, now it's all you: What is the one knock-'em-dead, blow-their-socks-off fan convention story that you haven't told us yet? It can be funny, sad, scary, sexy, heart-warming, terrifying, sexy, action packed, cerebral, sexy or gross. Did I mention it could be sexy?
My wife and I bought tickets to go to a fundraiser dinner to support the environmental cleanup of the Hudson River that was organized by the Kennedy family. Harrison Ford was the guest of honor to receive the Order of Patagonia for lifetime achievement. As always, people thought I was Jay

Leno. My wife suddenly told me not to turn around, but I did and slammed my shoulder into Harrison Ford while he was surrounded by microphones and being interviewed. I was blocked and couldn't move out of the shot, so I just nodded and agreed with everything he said. Later, he walked by me and I got a picture with him. This was 1999, just before the prequels started, and I asked him about them, but he wasn't involved in them. I shook his hand and was shocked he had a grip like a dead fish. I've run for office so I have a very firm grip, and he surprised me. Just then, a woman spilling out of her 20-year-old prom dress ran up and threw me her camera, an old 110, and told me to take her picture with Harrison Ford. She was all over him, so he was growling at me to hurry up. I've worked in advertising and know a lot about photography, but I couldn't figure out how to work this old camera. When I looked through the viewfinder, everything was black. The shutter button seemed to be in the wrong place, and I thought maybe it was a European model or something. Harrison Ford wanted me to hurry, so I just held the camera to my face close and pointed in their general direction. Everyone told me to stop, but it was too late. I had the camera backwards and the flash went off directly in my eye. I could see nothing but giant spots and was staggering around blind. Everyone was laughing at me. The woman was furious and called me an asshole. Harrison Ford and I kept passing the camera back and forth between us saying I don't want it, you take it. The woman insisted I try again, I said I couldn't see, and she said not to patronize her. My wife went off to get drunk on her own. I eventually found my wife and she said she couldn't believe I did that, and not to look because Harrison Ford was coming right at us. I thought he was going to kill me, but instead he gave me this strong, firm handshake and said that was the best picture he had ever had taken of himself, and all the lady got was a close-up of my retina. For the rest of the night, every time I got up, Harrison Ford would yell out "AND THAT'S THE GUY RIGHT THERE!" He even ended up in the valet line to get his big Toyota SUV right behind me while I was waiting for my little Camry with the child seat and the Winnie the Pooh window shade.

Have you had any international guests?

I've had people come from Germany and Australia. The Australian guy brought his wife and family. He came because he had never heard of a single show with so many classic comic artists and writers.

What keeps you going, organizing your shows per year, year after year?

Wanting to top myself every time. Every year, people expect more and more. It's like planning a wedding: you do all the work, but you don't actually see it. I'd love to go to one of my shows some time. People tell me they are fun.

They also get people together. As a result of a panel on Charlton Comics at one show, some friends of mine are making a documentary about the company. It was located in Derby, Connecticut, not far from where I live. One of the stories they found was that the comics were not supposed to be good. At one point, they were used to launder money for criminals, so the company started complaining when the quality of the books went up and started making a profit. They've interviewed tons of people who worked for Charlton, like John Byrne. When the founder of the company died and had an estate sale a couple of years ago, Byrne actually went because he wanted to buy the plaque that used to be in front of the building. He was willing to go as high as a thousand dollars, but they had already sold it for $300.

Inge Heyer

Inge Heyer is living proof that *The Big Bang Theory* may be a documentary. In addition to having a PhD in science education and a Master's in astronomy, she is co-chair of Shore Leave, a Baltimore area science fiction convention in its fortieth year. Run by the fans, Shore Leave is famous for its devotion to community service with its blood drives, food drives and cash donations to charity and for actually incorporating science programming into a science fiction convention. In addition to writing workshops and photo ops, it offers activities such as star gazing. Inge was inspired by

Star Trek to pursue her career path, and hopes science fiction continues to inspire others.

Can you give us a quick list of the fan conventions you have organized or appeared at, as both a fan and celebrity guest?
I have been attending conventions since 1982. I have been on the Shore Leave committee since 1992 and have been co-chair since 2012. I was a committee member of the 2007 SF Worldcon in Yokohama, Japan. I have been a science guest speaker (astronomy/physics) since 1993 at conventions all over the world (US, Canada, Japan, Germany, Poland, UK, Ireland).

What is the strangest thing you have seen asked to be autographed?
A car.

What is the sweetest or most touching thing a fan has said or done at one of your shows?
Many fans share their personal stories which often tell of perseverance in the face of great odds, made possible by the ideas and role models shown in SF (books and TV/movies). *Star Trek* is one such example, having inspired countless fans (including myself) to devote our lives to the sciences. I would not be an astronomy educator today if I hadn't started watching *Star Trek* at age 10. Most fans are very generous, emotionally and financially, in donating time, effort, and money to charitable causes. We collect a good amount of food, blood, and money every year at Shore Leave.

You interact with fans and vendors at conventions. What is the strangest thing someone has tried to sell at one of your shows?
The creativity of fans knows no bounds. I have seen many things in the Shore Leave dealers' room over the years that made me wish I'd thought of making that, some that made me wish I could afford that, and some that made me wish I could unsee that. Very new is the idea of 3-D printing, something that has certainly been mentioned in SF for ages, but that only recently has become reality. With the advent of SF-themed fabrics, amazing creations have popped up at vendors' tables, anything from purses to pants. The most beautiful thing I've ever seen was the Starship Enterprise made out of silver and turquoise (Zuni-style needlework).

What experiences have you had with fans who know far more about the celebrities of your various conventions than the celebrities themselves? How do various stars deal with that?

Shore Leave's media guests are very friendly and even-tempered, so they listen politely, and then, if necessary, redirect the conversation.

What is your average convention attendee like, and which person really surprised you by being a fan?

There is no such thing as an average convention attendee. Fandom's great strength is its diversity. Fans come from all walks of life. The beauty of a convention lies in that all these different people, who in everyday life would probably never meet, will sit together and participate in con activities. It allows everyone to experience new ideas and concepts. As an astronomer, I would never have thought I'd know anything about making movies or writing novels. But at conventions you get to learn new things every day.

What other celebrity encounters have you had at conventions? Feel free to tell us any funny, sexy and/or terrifying close encounters you have had.

We invite guests to Shore Leave that are known for being fan-friendly, in other words, people who are not afraid to chat and mingle. I have really not had any bad experiences with any of our guests. Some are fans themselves. Some are very generous and contribute significantly to our charity collections. Some may be a bit shy in the beginning, especially if it is their first convention, but by the end, everyone has a great time.

Cosplay has become an art form. What costume at any convention has totally blown you away and amazed you with its high quality and detail? What is the all-time worst costume you have seen?

I am blown away every year by the talent and creativity of the fans. Some are very good at sewing rich fabrics, and some can make really clever outfits with very simple and cheap stuff. I have seen costumes and make-up that rival professional work.

What super fans have you encountered whose whole lives have been consumed with one topic or movie they live for?

I have met many science-fiction fans who spent a lot of energy on their fandoms. But nobody does that to the exclusion of everything else. After all, we all have to earn a living, many of us have families, and many of us use what we have gained in fandom to teach the next generation of fans.

What about stars who aren't convention regulars or are appearing at their first show? Are they surprised by how strong their fandom is? How do they react to their first conventions?

Oh yes, the first-timers usually have very wide eyes when they encounter fandom for the first time. Even though they might have been told things by experienced colleagues, it is never the same as being at your first convention. I will never forget this senior NASA official turning very pale at the sight of his first Klingon in full battle gear. And there was the time when a scientist's laser pointer quit in the middle of her presentation and a Templar knight very politely offered his sword.

Fan conventions have gone from small gatherings to huge multi-media showcases. How has your show in particular changed and how has the type of celebrity who appears at them changed?

Shore Leave started out purely as a *Star Trek* convention in the late 70s. Over the decades we evolved into a media science fiction convention, covering all of science fiction in movies and TV. As a result, we now invite guests from all media SF (actors, authors, artists). However, we are still a fan-run, not-for-profit group, so our family-oriented programming and "family feel" has not changed.

Before you became a convention organizer, you were a fan. Ever have any true fanboy moments encountering celebrities before you became one of their employers?

Fanboy experiences no, fangirl experiences maybe. Having grown up with *Star Trek,* meeting any of the principals of any of the series or movies is truly an honor. Even after 50 years I still feel that way.

Photo ops are a convention favorite. Tell us about the more memorable ones you have seen.

Photo ops in most places are done assembly-line-style, so there isn't really a lot of interaction. The actors are always friendly, and some of them get creative and even silly, so I do have some photos that look… different.

Do you get many international fans at your shows, and how do they react to the North American version of anime and fandom?

Having travelled in five of the world's seven continents and met fans in all of them, I don't think the fans are all that different in other countries. They are creative and generous everywhere and usually go out of their way to make newcomers feel welcome.

Panels are a mainstay of conventions. Have you ever had one get out of hand? What happened? Which celebrities knew how to shut down hecklers?

Most fans know how to behave, so no, I do not know of a panel that went "out of control". That said, being that fandom is indeed very inclusive, we do have some folks that have less developed social skills. If someone asks inappropriate or off-topic questions, the panelists and/or the attending fans are usually very adept at redirecting without making anyone feel bad. A lot of work has gone into various areas of social awareness in fandom in recent years, and I think the stereotypical idea of the socially clueless male as the typical fan is no longer applicable.

Do fans ever confuse the actor with the characters they portray?

Very young ones, probably.

What would be your dream guest in the future?

Anyone who brings in lots of enthusiastic convention attendees, makes them cheer and laugh, and generally has a positive attitude towards fandom.

OK, now it's all you: what is the one knock-'em-dead, blow-their-socks-off fan convention story that you haven't told us yet? It can be funny, sad, scary, sexy, heart-warming, terrifying, sexy, action-packed, cerebral, sexy, or gross. Did I mention it could be sexy?

It is not one particular story that stands out, but the sum of my experiences over 50 years of fandom. Without this family of friends, known and unknown, my life would indeed have been not only very different, but a whole lot less rich.

What keeps you going, organizing shows, year after year?

Seeing the happy faces of the fans after the convention and hearing them say how much they enjoyed it.

The danger of asking for a replacement laser pointer at a science fiction convention

Doug Jones

The youngest of four brothers, Doug Jones was born on May 24, 1960 in Indianapolis, Indiana, and grew up in the city's North East side. After attending Bishop Chatard High School, he headed off to Ball State University, where he graduated in 1982 with a Bachelor's degree in Telecommunications, with a minor in Theatre. He learned mime at school, joining a troupe and doing the whole white-face thing, and has also worked as a contortionist.

After a hitch in theater in Indiana, he moved to Los Angeles in 1985, and has not been out of work since - he's acted in over 25 films, many television series (Including the award-winning *Buffy the Vampire Slayer* (1997), his episode 'Hush' garnered two Emmy nominations) and over 90 commercials and music videos with the likes of Madonna and Marilyn Manson. Although known mostly for his work under prosthetics, he has also performed as 'himself' in such highly-rated films as *Adaptation* (2002) with Nicolas Cage and indie projects such as Phil Donlon's *A Series of Small Things* (2005). But it is his sensitive and elegant performance as 'Abe Sapien' in *Hellboy* (2004), which stormed to the top of the U.S. box office in the spring of 2004, which has brought him an even higher profile and much praise from audiences and critics alike. Doug is married and lives in California.

Can you give us a quick list of the fan conventions you have appeared at as a celebrity guest?
I have been doing shows consistently for 11 years, so there are too many to name.

What is the strangest thing you have been asked to autograph?

A woman's forearm. That in itself isn't that weird, but she came back a couple of hours later, and she had just had a tattoo done over my autograph. It was still red and bloody. I was shocked and told her she was stuck with that for the rest of her life. She said that at least I was in good company and showed me a Stan Lee autograph on her other forearm. I just had visions of her passing away sometime in the future, lying in her casket with her arms crossed, and her whole family will think I was involved in some weird love triangle.

Have you had people come up to you dressed as one of your characters?

All the time. I love it. Many of them are aspiring makeup artists and they come with professional looking costumes and makeup. It is the world's greatest compliment when that happens.

What experiences have you had with fans who know far more about your career than you could ever hope to know? How do you deal with that situation?

That happens at every show. It is a little embarrassing when someone comes up reciting all the dialogue from some bad movie that I did in the 80's that I am desperately trying to forget.

Have you ever been mistaken for someone else at a convention, and thought "why the Hell did you think I was them?"

Not really, but people have told me that I look like David Bowie or Bruce Willis. I've had to shave my head for my latest role, so I look different now.

If I had an eyebrow pencil to draw in a thin moustache, I'd look exactly like John Waters.

You have been interviewed and done panels at conventions. What are the funniest, strangest and most thought provoking questions you have encountered?

There are no bad questions, but the ones I get frustrated with are the ones that go on and on about makeup techniques. I am not a makeup artist. I am an all-around actor. Let's talk about acting.

Sarah Karloff

Sara Karloff is the daughter of the legendary Boris Karloff and is a veteran convention guest. An absolute delight to interview, she is an extremely polite, knowledgeable and well-spoken individual. She is also humble to a fault. When I referred to her as horror royalty, she was very quick to correct me and explain to me in no uncertain terms that I was not to do so, as it was her father who was horror royalty, and not her, and that she represents his legacy and not herself. If you get a chance to meet her and attend a panel she is part of, make sure that you do, but be careful to ask for her signature, and not her autograph.

Can you give us a quick list of the fan conventions you have appeared at as a celebrity guest?

I have appeared at the fall Chiller Theatre show every year for the last twenty-four years. Kevin Clement, one of the organizers, is wonderful to me. I have been a guest at every one of the spring Monsterpalooza's since the second one. I've been to Scarecon, and other shows too numerous to mention.

What is the strangest thing you have been asked to autograph?

I was appearing at The WItch's Dungeon years ago in Bristol, CT. It was freezing outside, and I was huddled in a trailer trying to keep warm. A lady in her 60's came running up to me saying that her son wanted me to sign something. He eventually came along, and he was in his thirties. He was a big man, but he was no bodybuilder. Even though it was freezing, he proceeded to take off his shirt. He wanted me to sign one of his love handles. This was the first time I had ever been asked to sign a body part. I told him I would do it, but then he could never shower or bathe again, and he said he had already planned on never doing that again anyway.

I always tell people that I never autograph anything. My father autographed things. What they get from me is a signature. My signature is not going to enhance the value of anything. I will refuse to sign certain valuable objects, like certain posters, because my signature will only detract from its value. It can be hard to make fans understand that, but if I ever lose sight of that I'd be better off if I just stayed home and cleaned my oven.

What is the most inappropriate thing a fan has done or said to you?

I want to stress that no fan has ever been inappropriate with me. Some of the requests may have been a little unusual, like the love handle story, but convention fans have never been anything but nice and polite to me. I am always treated with such amazing respect. Nothing negative has ever been written or said about my father, and his fans are very deferential to his legacy. Their questions are never inappropriate or prying.

When I was a child I went to private girls' schools. We wore uniforms and white shoes, and were told that only cheap girls pierce their ears. Until

I started going to fan conventions, I had never seen so many pierced and painted body parts, and many of these great people have become my best friends.

What about the flipside? What is the sweetest or most touching thing a fan has said or done for you?

There are far too many examples to select just one. People are always bringing me incredible gifts, life photos autographed by my father. One fan brought me a collection of letters that he had written to my grand-mother when he was on Broadway doing the play *Arsenic and Old Lace.* He had bought them at an auction. Some very gifted artists have given me beautiful, framed art of my father and his characters. One year a friend gave me his collection of all of the issues of the comic book *Boris Karloff Tales of Mystery* as well as playbills of the five plays he did on Broadway.

I have a room in my home called The Bathing with Boris Bathroom. The counter is covered with Karloff models and sculptures and the walls are covered with photographs of my father. I did not buy anything in the room. Everything is a gift from his fans.

The best sculptures of my father have been done by the great artist Mike Hill. The best paintings of him and his characters were by Basil Gogos, whom I knew quite well. His art was totally unique and he used incredibly vivid colors.

Have you had people come up to you dressed as one of your father's characters?

Many times, almost always as Frankenstein or the Mummy.

When I was at the Calgary comic book convention, a 400 pound guy stepped on my foot and I yelled out "Jesus Christ!" A cosplayer dressed as Jesus Christ (at least I think it was a cosplayer) promptly appeared and offered to heal me. What is your personal WTF story from any convention?

That is a funny story, but I really don't have an equivalent. If I make an irreverent comment to make, I make it to myself. There was one show I did in the Deep South, and due to the diet down there, everyone who attended was completely round. I was tempted to make a comment, but I kept it to myself.

What experiences have you had with fans who know far more about your father's career than you could ever hope to know? How do you deal with that situation?

I am grateful for those fans. I learn something new about my father every single time I attend a convention because his fans are more informed than I could ever hope to be. I receive seventy-five emails a day, and many of them are questions about my father that I can't answer, but I have a very select group of his fans that I can turn to and pass their answers on to answer the email. I always make it clear that I am getting the answer from one of these fans.

What other celebrity encounters have you had at conventions? Feel free to tell us any funny, sexy and/or terrifying close encounters you have had.

I don't talk about celebrities that I meet, but I can tell you that my father has had some very surprising celebrity fans. Hugh Hefner, the founder of Playboy, was a great fan of my father and had a life-size statue of Frankenstein in the foyer of Playboy Mansion West. Kirk Hammett, the lead guitarist of Metallica, is a great fan and has become a great friend. He is a very nice, soft- spoken family man. The director Gullermo del Toro, is not only a great fan of my father but has a huge collection of monster film memorabilia. Peter Bogdanovich, the director and film historian, is not only a great fan of my father but directed my father in my favorite film, *Targets*.

Cosplay has become an art form. What costume at any convention has totally blown you away and amazed you with its high quality and detail? What is the all-time worst costume you have seen?

There are so many wonderful costumes. Some of them are of professional quality.

You have been photographed thousands of times. What is your favorite photo with a fan?

I will not name names, but so many well-known celebrities who are also convention guests have jumped up and had their pictures taken with me, then had me sit at their tables and tell me stories about my father.

Gender bender cosplay continues to get more and more popular. Have you met a female version of your father's character at conventions?
Never. If his female fans dress up, it is always as the bride of Frankenstein.

Before you became a celebrity you were a fan. Ever have any true fangirl moments encountering celebrities before you became one?
I have never been a fawning fan. However, I love getting celebrity autographs for the children of my assistant.

You have been interviewed and done panels at conventions. What are the funniest, strangest and most thought provoking questions you have encountered?
I have done many panels, but I consider myself to be there as a fluff piece and not a serious scholar. I do show home movies and old interviews of my father. Panels are usually topic driven, so the questions are never funny. Some of my answers can be funny and very irreverent, but I can't think of any examples off the top of my head. I feel very fortunate to be invited to take part in panels and am always happy to participate.

In terms of other interviews, I prefer being interviewed in person or by telephone rather than by email. In email interviews, there is little candour. In live interviews, there is a great personal interaction with the interviewer.

The strangest question I ever received was not in a formal interview but in a telephone call from Madame Tussaud's in London. They wanted to know if there was one or two buttons on Frankenstein's fly flap. I'm not sure why I would ever know that, so I deferred to a very expert fan to answer that one.

Have you been to any foreign conventions?
Many in both England and Germany. I have never been to a Japanese convention but would like to be invited there one day.

You are often on the road. What is the hardest part about travel, and your funniest story from being on the road?
My travel arrangements are arranged by convention organizers. They take incredible care of me and make sure nothing goes wrong. I'm sorry, but that doesn't make for any funny stories.

OK, now it's all you: What is the one knock-'em-dead, blow-their-socks-off fan convention story that you haven't told us yet? It can be funny, sad, scary, sexy, heart-warming, terrifying, action packed, cerebral, sexy or gross.

Other than what I have already told you, none. But I would like to say that I am there to represent my father's legacy and not to glorify myself or be the center of attention. I love it when people know that he was so much more than a horror icon. He was one of the founding members of the Screen Actors Guild and his card number was 9. He has been honored on three United States postage stamps, and fans have told me that is a number only equalled by some U.S. presidents. The Postal Office has been wonderful to work with. He played Captain Hook and Mr. Darling in *Peter Pan* on Broadway. He loved doing comedy and loved doing two films with Abbott and Costello (*Abbott and Costello meet the Killer Boris Karloff* and *Abbott and Costello meet Dr. Jekyll and Mr. Hyde*). He did two movies with Jack Nicholson, *The Terror* and *The Raven*. *The Terror* was Nicholson's first film. He loved doing *The Raven* and *Comedy of Terrors*. Peter Lorre and Vincent Price were in both, and Basil Rathbone was in *Comedy of Terrors*. They were great friends. Those old men had a great time, spoofing their old characters and playing pranks, but they drove Roger Corman crazy.

Liana Kerzner

This book is targeted at fans who attend fan conventions. Even if you are not a fan of Liana K for some reason I will never understand, accept the fact that she is right when she says women at conventions deserve better treatment. Below are pictures of Liana with the character she wrote and co-starred with for years, Ed the Sock, as well as the title of one of her You Tube videos.

Can you give us a quick list of the fan conventions you have appeared at, as both a fan and celebrity guest?

I've been to a bunch of conventions across the US and Canada. I'm not sure how many of the smaller ones are still around. I think Ad Astra is still around. Keycon in Winnipeg. And of course, the big ones like San Diego

Comicon, Fan Expo, Ottawa Comicon, Anime North, Calgary Comic and Entertainment Expo. G-Anime in Ottawa is another one I've been to. I was in Baltimore for Baltimore Comic-Con, but got sick and never actually saw the convention. The best time I remember having at a convention was at Pure Spec Edmonton. I made friends at that convention I still keep in contact with. I don't do as many conventions lately, because it's just gotten too expensive, and I was recovering from a knee injury. But I have a few new costumes now that I could take for a spin.

What is the strangest thing you have been asked to autograph?

I have a high bar for strange, so I can't really think about anything that I found odd. For three years in a row, I did a cosplay of a Frank Cho character, and he signed my butt. But that was my idea. Frank is actually shy in his own way, so I told him I'd only cosplay Shanna the She-Devil if he signed my butt like a Cabbage Patch Kid. I don't think either of us thought the other would go through with it! But it became a yearly thing. The next year was Ms Marvel, then it was a double butt signing with me dressed as Brandy from Liberty Meadows and another female Cho fan as Jen. I loved that costume. The shoes were Keds! So comfortable!

What is the most inappropriate thing a fan has done or said to you?

The people who are inappropriate are not really fans. I've had my share of bad experiences -- groping, minor assault, stuff like that. The weirdest one was when someone took my picture in a bathroom while I was gluing on a mask. I almost lost it on that one. It's a damned bathroom! Don't take photos in the damned bathroom!

What about the flipside? What is the sweetest or most touching thing a fan has said or done for you?

I have a lot of great stories. I still have every picture a kid drew me at a convention. I love the kid stuff. Overall, I'm struck by the openness of the creators at conventions. Comic book professionals are a pretty approachable bunch.

Have you had people come up to you dressed as one of your characters (i.e. one you are also cosplaying)? Does it get competitive or is it all just part of the fun?

If a character gets more popular, I retire the costume, so it doesn't get competitive. The exception to that is Poison Ivy, because there are so many variations. Two Ivy costumes can be totally different, so it's less of an awkward thing.

When I was at the Calgary comic book convention, a 400 pound guy stepped on my foot and I yelled out "Jesus Christ!" A cosplayer dressed as Jesus Christ (at least I think it was a cosplayer) promptly appeared and offered to heal me. What is your personal WTF story from any convention?

Stuff like that is the fun of conventions! I guess the closest I can come to that was when the provincial Conservative Party leadership convention (Like Canada's Republicans) had their convention at the same building as Anime North. There were a bunch of delegates -- of course in blue suits -- walking toward me and my friend. She was dressed as Sophitia and I was Ivy Valentine from Soulcalibur. It got awkward and to break the ice, I blurted out "Hi guys! Does this costume uphold conservative values?" One guy gave a very sllooooooooow thumbs up, and the cosplayers around us all laughed.

You are a model, cosplayer, actress, writer and You Tuber. Are people surprised you are so talented? Do they expect you to be one thing but not the others?

They expect me to be dumb, slutty and insecure, which is disappointing.

What experiences have you had with fans who know far more about you than you could expect them to know? How do you deal with that situation?

Being on TV, I got used to people knowing way more about me than I knew about them. I just try to be the best listener I can and ask a lot of questions.

What other celebrity encounters have you had at conventions? Feel free to tell us any funny, sexy and/or terrifying close encounters you have had.

I love the original Ghostbusters, so I HAD to meet Ernie Hudson. The day I could go over to talk to him, I happened to be in my metal Princess Leia bikini. I asked him how much an autograph was, and he said, "Well, normally it's thirty dollars but most people don't ask me dressed like you!" I laughed and said, "So it's an exchange of services, is it?" He nodded, then signed the picture with the caption "That's a big Twinkie." In the #metoo era, I'm sure some people are shocked or horrified by that, but it was fun. It was all totally okay for everyone involved. I don't tend to approach celebrities, so that was a fun one.

Have you ever been mistaken for someone else at a convention, and thought "why the Hell did you think I was them?" It can be either mistaking you for someone else, mistaking your character for someone else, or both.

I get confused for Jessica Nigri sometimes, and that's really weird. Jessica is teeny tiny and much younger than me. Super cool though. I cosplay obscure characters, so I expect a lot of people to get it wrong.

Cosplay has become an art form. What costume at any convention has totally blown you away and amazed you with its high quality and detail? What is the all-time worst costume you have seen?

There's been a lot of great work. Some of the Worbla armor blows me away because I suck with Worbla. I stick to Wonderflex. I love any Overwatch character cosplay. Mel Colley made a Zenyatta costume that was ASTOUNDING.

You have been photographed thousands of times. What is your favorite photo with a fan, and what was the one request that made you shake your head, laugh or throw up a little in your mouth?

I like the fetishy ones. I wouldn't have the balls to ask for pictures like that, so I find those ones fun. I know that's weird, but I like the vulnerability inherent in someone sharing something like that. The ones I HATE are the ones where someone uses a photo to grope me or force a kiss on me. I wish

I could punch those guys in the face. Or the balls. The fetish types ASK. They get consent. That's cool. The guys who just grope...opposite of cool.

Gender bender cosplay continues to get more and more popular. Have you met a male version of you at conventions? What was that like? Have you done gender bender?

I cosplayed the Mad Hatter. The Johnny Depp one. That was fun. I also did kind of a gender bend Kratos. I want to do a costume based on a particular comic where Plastic-Man disguised himself as Big Barda's dress. I'm not sure what would qualify as a male version of me at a convention. Other than the guys who wear the Leia bikinis!

Before you became a celebrity you were a fan. Ever have any true fangirl moments encountering celebrities before you became one?

I'm a bad fangirl. I'm too shy to approach celebrities I'm a fan of. I had a few early bad experiences when I worked at Muchmusic -- I'm looking at YOU, Smashing Pumpkins -- and decided to avoid it from that point on. Though I was part of a Mark Hamill interview for work and that guy is the best guy ever. He's the best. SO nice. Stan Lee was also a huge amount of fun to meet. I met Christina Aguilera a few times and she was always really sweet. Her reputation as a diva in the press is a combination of a manufactured narrative and people not understanding how damned hard it is to sing the way she does.

Have you been interviewed and done panels at conventions? What are the funniest, strangest and most thought provoking questions you have encountered?

I've done a lot of panels but the one I'm most proud of is the panel on Steve Ditko I was a part of at San Diego Comicon. Ditko's art was visionary, but he was his own worst enemy, and I'm glad that comic book historians have embraced both elements of him.

Have you done any foreign conventions yet? What was that like?

Do American ones count? Nothing outside of North America. I'd love to go to a convention in Britain.

You are constantly on the road. What is the hardest part about travel, and your funniest story from being on the road?

Daytona with a camera man drunk off his ass on Wild Turkey!

OK, now it's all you: What is the one knock-'em-dead, blow-their-socks-off fan convention story that you haven't told us yet? It can be funny, sad, scary, sexy, heart-warming, terrifying, sexy, action packed, cerebral, sexy or gross. Did I mention it could be sexy?

We had a little person airbrush body paint a nude model for charity once. True story. There are pics. The little person was my friend, a really great stand-up comedian named Andre Arruda who has since passed away. Andre and I had good times at conventions together. He was a student of the absurd. He's also actually the reason I no longer have a Playstation 3. I loaned it to him in the hospital, along with a bunch of my games, because he was bored. I assumed I'd get it back from him eventually, but he died. Never made it out of the hospital. I swear he knew somehow. But all those crazy experiences we had at conventions together, many of which involved booze and nudity, mean a lot more now, because he had such limited time. I can say I was part of him living the life he had to the fullest.

You are a pro cosplayer, and a damn good one. What tips do you have for fans who aren't at your level?

I don't see it as a "level" thing. It' a fun thing, and a personal exploration thing. Don't be afraid to get help or pay for commissions. It doesn't make you less of a cosplayer. It's a way to learn. I learned a lot of the stuff I did through the process of paying better technicians to work with me. More and more, I built up my skills. I am actually really conflicted about the way cosplay has gone pro. It's a lifestyle to me. A way of navigating the world. Costume helps us contextualize our experience. I'm actually really shy and introverted, and cosplay helps me a lot in knowing how to behave in various situations.

Some of your writing, such as your position on feminism and gaming, have been controversial. Do you get any haters at conventions? Supporters? How do you deal?

I do get haters, but they usually get me blacklisted from conventions so there haven't been that many confrontations. Some of them did get scary. Like, stalker scary. But most people are crazy in a fun way instead of crazy in a good way. I don't seek controversy. My views are only controversial because there's a profound lack of authenticity out there, so when someone speaks their mind, people freak out. No way through that but forward. I deal by having a lot of cats. Cats keep you humble, but they also remind you that it IS possible to lick your own butt and still seem regal and dignified.

Ken Kish

Cinema Wasteland is Ken Kish. Ken Kish is a legend.

To be slightly more specific, Cinema Wasteland fan conventions are held twice yearly in Cleveland, Ohio. These shows are highly regarded in the movie fan community. Although the show's organizer, Ken Kish, doesn't like the "horror movie" convention label, he is famous for bringing in such legends as George Romero, the cast of *Night of the Living Dead*, scream queens like Brinke Stevens and Veronica Hart, horror icons like P.J. Soles and Dyanne Thorne and cast members of *The Hills Have Eyes* and *Dawn of the Dead*. The shows cover a wide range of cinema subjects, from exploitation to family classics like *E.T.*

The shows are organized by Ken Kish. Ken is famous in fan circles for being outspoken and a true fan, not just a fly by night charlatan who is currently organizing fan conventions since he was released from prison for selling counterfeit New Kids on the Block merchandise.

Ken also runs the Cinema Wasteland store. Check them out online for a great selection of hard-to-find movies, autographs, memorabilia and body parts.

No, that is not fanboy slang for something else. Actual body parts.

Why is Ken Kish a legend? How many convention organizers have their own IMDb page? How many convention organizers get singled out by an industry legend like Dyanne Thorne as being their favorite convention organizer of all time? Who else could make this beard and moustache combo look this good?

Can you give us a quick list of the fan conventions you have organized or appeared at, as both a fan and celebrity guest?
Although I've helped several people with their conventions over the years, I try not to tell anybody what to do. I'm just there if I can help out a friend. If they have a question I may have an answer for, I'll answer it honestly. If I can run a panel in a pinch, I'll run the panel. If they need somebody to screen a couple of films, then I'm that guy.

I save my energies for my own show, The Cinema Wasteland Movie and Memorabilia Expo, a celebration of the drive-in era of films. There, I do everything from invite the guests, to run the panels, pick the films, and schedule all 60+ hours of Movie, Panels, and Programming fans can enjoy over a three-day weekend.

And even if they wanted to, I've never let anybody call me a guest. I've written a couple of movie review books, but I don't consider myself an author. I've been making money on my art since I was 13 years old, but I don't consider myself an artist. I've appeared in independent films in small roles, but I don't consider myself an actor. I've done lectures on the rise and fall of the drive-in theatre, the glory days of "Mom and Pop" video stores, but I don't consider myself an expert. I'm just a fan. And anything I've ever accomplished is for myself. I don't think I look cool because I've done them and I don't feel the need to brag about it. I have zero ambition to claim my fifteen minutes of fame.

What is the strangest thing you have seen someone ask to have autographed?"
I never find any of it strange, but you name it. I've seen people have their
own body autographed so they can go and get it tattooed in later, I've seen
women have their breasts autographed for no apparent reason. I've seen
some of the worst fan art imaginable and/or the most tattered book or
magazine signed... It's all personal to somebody, so none of it is strange
to me. I myself tricked George Romero into signing an actual human
skull back in 1993. I had to trick him because he would never sign human
bones. And I didn't want his standard "Stay Scared" notation he's signed
on thousands of things written on it, so it's signed, "The One That Got
Away!"

*What is the most inappropriate thing a fan has done or said at one of your
conventions? What about a celebrity guest?*
Sadly you'll never go broke underestimating the stupidity of the human
race, so I've heard it all - from fans as well as guests of the show. But it's
just dumb shit that falls out of their mouths and the kinds of things you'd
overhear at any given lunch counter. Everything from racist comments - I
had an alcoholic guest once that I almost beat the hell out of because I
heard him slinging racists remarks around - but mostly you hear the racist
remarks down south and can easily ignore it. I overheard somebody asking
a woman who just had had a mastectomy when her baby was due because,
well, she just had her breasts removed and wasn't a small woman to begin
with. But-none of it shakes me. It's just people saying stuff people say.

*What about the flip-side? What is the sweetest or most touching thing a fan
has said or done at one of your shows?*
At my show we've had five or six actual weddings over the years and a few
public proposals on stage before events take place. Everyone in attendance
at the show was invited every time we had a wedding and it's always fun
when family members show up expecting something a little more tradi-
tional. Herschell Gordon Lewis, "The Godfather of Gore", even gave the
bride away once. I ran my second show three days after 9-11 and actually
had vendors pick up and drive guests to the show when no planes could
get off the ground. I've had fans help take care of guests in a pinch, watched
nervous fans pace around wanting to deliver a bouquet of flowers to a guest
they've always admired, and somebody rushing to the aid of a stumbling

drunk in need of his or her hotel room bed before they hit the floor. It's the little things that make me smile.

You interact with fans not only through your conventions but as a vendor of horror films and memorabilia. What is the strangest thing a fan has tried to sell you or request from you?

I've bought and sold any and everything I thought I could sell in my 30+ years of buying and selling (mostly movie memorabilia) so there isn't anything I've ever found strange in the least. I've sold human skulls, serial killer artwork and autographs, really big bugs, things in a jar, shrunken heads, and ring quality Mexican wrestling masks I used to have made in Mexico to name just a few of the more unusual things I've sold over the years. In all honesty, I'd sell something I ran over on the way to the show if I thought somebody would give me a dollar for it, so I actively look for unusual stuff to sell that isn't my normal line of products.

Horror films include several sub-genres, like classic Universal films, slasher movies, dead teenager movies, drive-in shlock, etc. How do fans of different sub-genres interact with each other? Have you seen any funny or shocking confrontations between fans over the years?

Fans get along pretty well as far as I've witnessed over the years. Until the mid-2000s, there were only a dozen actual horror conventions running in the country. Before the year 2000, there were fewer than 7 or 8 I know of. So you had comic book shows, western shows, and movie memorabilia shows that didn't bring in guests. I wasn't into old cowboy and Indian westerns, so I set up as the odd man out any show except western shows and found that there was a lot of cross-interest along the way.

Pretty much anyone over the age of 45 started out as a classic monster movie fan, and if their interests broadened into slasher films or newer horror films, so be it. Comic book fans like movies, and movie fans like comics. But not every comic fan is into horror films or horror comics either. Everyone has a favorite movie and will buy the original poster for it if it's affordable.

The only thing I see fans getting prickly about has happened in the last few years. Nobody likes the clueless fan who didn't attend a convention until last year and feels the need to get in your damn way, or take pictures of everything to stick on their stupid fucking Facebook page. Take it from me… more people would like to shove your selfie stick up your ass than be caught dead within six feet of you holding it. And I'm not the only person who hates fair-weather fans who hop on the latest bandwagon just because some douchebag on the internet says it's cool. Those kinds of fans have always been around, and most recently, everyone knows or has met a completely clueless Walking Dead fan who thinks they know everything about the zombie genre but don't have the slightest clue who George Romero is and has never seen a single classic Italian zombie movie. To anybody who's ever been caught in a conversation with one of them, I feel for you man, I really do. LOL

When I was at the Calgary comic book convention, a 400 pound guy stepped on my foot and I yelled out "Jesus Christ!" A cosplayer dressed as Jesus Christ (at least I think it was a cosplayer) promptly appeared and offered to heal me. What is your personal WTF story from any convention?

After attending comic book conventions since I was a kid in the mid-1970's and on through becoming a convention vendor in the late 1980's and running my own show for the last 17 years, I could fill a book with personal stories about my life on the road. Both good and not-so-good. From sober to completely plowed. From very funny to extremely tragic. I'm full of stories. And I've been asked to write them down and turn them into a book many times when I start telling a couple of them to people, so maybe one day I will. But for now, I could never answer that question in only a couple of sentences I'm sorry to say.

What experiences have you had with fans who know far more about the themes of your various conventions than you would expect them to know? How do you deal with that situation?

I prefer a knowledgeable fan over a know-it-all fan any day of the week and have come across both more times than I can count.

When I make a mistake on a guest bio for my show or when writing up a quick movie description or even writing a full-length movie review, it's never long before I'm corrected by somebody if I make a mistake. I don't have much of an ego, so I appreciate the correction as long as the person correcting me isn't an asshole about it.

Know-it-all fans are the flip side of the coin, and as a fan myself, I find them annoying because most often they are flat-out wrong but douchebag enough to demand they're right. A know-it-all movie fan is exactly like the creepy Christians who want to tell you what the Bible says and how to lead your life but have never actually read the Bible they quote from. There should be a law that says it's OK to cut the tongues out of their mouths so nobody has to ever hear the sound of their voice ever again. I guess it's a good thing I'm not in charge of making the laws in this country...?

What is your average convention attendee like, and which person really surprised you by being a fan?

As far as the Cinema Wasteland Movie and Memorabilia Expo goes, most attending fans are movie fans that know their stuff when it comes to "B" films from the late 1950's through the 1980's.

And it always surprises me when a guest is actually a fan of what it is we celebrate at the CW Show. Above all, we celebrate "B" movies, and all actors find themselves in a few of them but not all are fans of them. To find a guest that enjoys sitting in on the late-night movies we screen or sitting in on some other guest's talk or panel is always cool to me.

Generally speaking, the fans that will make a road trip to attend any show are generous people who like to interact with other people. They enjoy the whole experience that fandom offers and only attend conventions featuring things they are fans of.

What about haters? Have people come to your conventions just to say how much they hate horror or your particular guests?

I don't run a horror movie show. I run a "B" Movie Show. A "Drive-In" movie show for lack of a better way to state it, so we don't just celebrate horror films. We celebrate everything that was popular at the drive-in from adult movies to horror films, spaghetti westerns, comedies, and oddball indie stuff from the late 60's and 70's, from that slice of time where Hollywood actually put out original films rather than the same stale old shit they go back to rehashing time and time again.

But, to answer your question, no, the haters don't actually attend the show. The know-it-all assholes and trolls who don't actually know much about anything but have an opinion about everything are generally all found on the internet these days. They used to wander into the occasional convention and whine like, say, a 70-year-old, thin-skinned, Cheeto-colored grown man with tiny hands who acts like a thirteen-year-old girl; then leave the show so you could laugh about them with other vendors who got stuck listening to them whine, but I don't see them any longer. And before the internet they used to write letters, and somehow I lost them over the years... probably in a move? But I used to save them and wanted to publish a book of them. I would have if I still had them or could find them.

Other than the golden age whiners and the amusing letters, I've run 30 shows in 17 years and my favorite line from somebody who has never attended my show is always, "I'd attend your convention if you'd get (insert a guest you can see at 75 other cons a year for the last 8 or 10 years here) as a guest"... Yeah. Right.

What other celebrity encounters have you had at conventions? Feel free to tell us any funny, sexy and/or terrifying close encounters you have had.

Out of all the actors and various guests I've met at conventions over the years I've made a ton of friends, but I don't do the cult of celebrity and don't tell stories about friends. What some consider a "celebrity" I consider just people - oftentimes just as dumb as the next person you'll meet, with the same hang-ups, family, spouse, and/or emotional problems we all have. I can tell a million stories. Some of them are sad, others funny, and lots of them are personal. It's hard to name names because I tease the homophobic celebrities I know, pester the assholes I know, shake my head at the people I know that are cheating on their spouse with some show whore, get under the skin of the people who think they're something other than a person doing their job like anybody else who goes to work every day, and know far too many personal stories about actors I've become friends with. I'm like the Las Vegas slogan. What Ken knows, stays with Ken. Unless of course you shout it for the world to hear, like when I walked past the late drug addict Corey Haim shouting, "I have the money, now bring me an eight ball" into his clunky cell phone in the middle of a crowded convention floor in Chicago...

OK, I can tell one common story since it happens often enough to us and he wouldn't mind if I told it... Me and my wife, Pam, have known Michael Berryman for too many years to count now and he's become a pretty good friend over the years, so we tend to go out to eat dinner a lot when we see each other at various conventions around the country. Hotel food gets old, so we will go searching for some good non-corporate restaurant. Michael Berryman isn't a guy who can walk into a place unnoticed. He looks like

Michael Berryman 24-7. But the guy never wants any sort of special treatment. Now, if I've been to the place before or if he's in Cleveland, it's easy for me to ask for a table in a corner or away from foot traffic so we can get some peace during our meal. But that's not always the case, so, it never fails... There we are at a table in the middle of the restaurant and before you know it, people start looking over at us. Then, somebody will get up the nerve to walk over and ask for a photo or an autograph. Mike will never tell anybody "no" and I won't yell at them for him unless we are in the middle of our meal. I always tell him that if he wants me to, I'll play the bad guy and shoo them off. Unless it gets bad and I just do it, he will eventually wind up meeting the staff, getting names and an address and sending off a small stack of photos to the restaurant a week later. He's gotten dragged into wedding parties and started lines of people in restaurants. But, by the same token, he's gotten us free drinks, free desserts, and a lot of apologies from owners who catch wind of what's going on and race out to say hello. Michael takes it all in stride. He doesn't crave attention, but he realizes he is who he is and fans will recognize him so he has a good time playing along and I've never seen it go to his head.

Have you ever been mistaken for someone else at a convention, and thought "why the hell did you think I was him?" Have you had any celebrity guests mistaken for other people?

Oddly enough, I look like somebody everyone between the age of 45 and 55 knows or went to school with. I have been stopped in any given city in any given state at any given time for the last 30 years by strangers who think I'm somebody else. I always play along. I've had twenty minute conversations with complete strangers in a grocery store in some odd state I was in for the weekend about what's been happening to whoever they think I am since high school. My wife just stands there shaking her head and if whoever I'm talking to about the past life we never had together notices her, I drag her into the conversation, usually telling them not to say anything to anybody about running into me "because we're both married and well, you know..." knowing full well they will now go out and tell everyone whoever they thought I was is cheating on his wife.

In the early-to-mid-1990's I was mistaken for an indie wrestler dozens of times. I'm 6'3" and weighed in at 240 pounds or so back then, so it was easy to see. Plus, I'd always be wearing indie wrestling promotion tee-shirts because a ton of guys I knew ran indie promotions. Depending on the person and just how happy they were to see whoever they thought I was, I'd stop for a photo (back in the day you had to carry a small camera around at shows to get photos) and always ask them who they saw me wrestle as so I could slap them in whatever signature move the wrestler used. You can say I'm like Santa Claus. I just like to make strangers happy.

Me and a buddy once convinced a couple kids we were Jabba the Hut's tail. There've always been those convention guests that are so marginal that who really gives a shit about them… and who the hell would pay them for an autograph? Star Wars was one of the worst, so, hey, we gave the kid a free autograph when others just as worthless "celebrities" were charging for them. Just like Santa Claus I tell ya!

What is the one that got away? Which celebrity were you this close to getting only to have them pull out at the last nanosecond?

I've held more first-time reunions and brought in more first-time convention guests than any other convention I've seen (except for the Chiller Theatre convention, who brought in a ton of first time guests back in the 1990s), so I can't say I've ever had somebody "get away". To me, a yes is as good as a no once you get hold of somebody and invite them to attend my show. The sin is being too lazy to hunt them down and invite them in the first place. But overall, I've surprised myself more often than not and tend to have first-time guests at every one of my shows, so I'll just keep on keeping on and hope I continue to uncover first-time guests that fit what it is we're all about.

The exception is death. I've had a few older people die after I invited them but before they actually made the show. That kind of sucked because I was looking forward to showing them a good time. But, on the other hand, I've had more than my share of older guests that passed away after they attended my show so I was able to show them a good time before they passed away.

Cosplay has become an art form. What costume at any convention has totally blown you away and amazed you with its high quality and detail? What is the all-time worst costume you have seen?

Fans dress up. They have the entire time I've been doing conventions. I appreciate fans who want to have fun and put their time into a costume no matter how much or how little actual talent they have in creating it. If they are having fun, I'm having fun right along with them.

I can't say I actually hate cosplay. People get into it and it's fun for them, so who is anyone to judge somebody else if they are having a good time? What I hate is "cosplay people" thinking they're some sort of celebrity... or worse yet, seeing them listed as a guest somewhere like people really give a shit who they are. I've certainly never met a single person who told me they need to go and meet some cosplay person anywhere - ever. To me they are fans. Just like any other fan who enjoys dressing up at a convention. They just seem to have a creepy need to stand in everyone's way so random other fans can take a picture of or with them. But as a vendor, costumes don't have pockets, and we all know you don't have any money, so get the hell away from my table or booth space to take your damn photos, please.

A buddy of mine is good at sculpting and casting latex. He'd never in a million years call himself a "cosplayer" because I think he'd feel the term was just as dumb as I do, but he's actually created full-size Godzilla or big monster costumes that weigh a hundred pounds or more and are horrible to wear, BUT, they are the best things I've ever seen! It sure beats seeing 57 people dressed as Ash from *Evil Dead* in every costume contest I see. Yeah, like yet another Ash is sooooooo original after 35 years of seeing fans dressed like him.

What super fans have you encountered whose whole lives have been consumed with one topic or movie they live for?
I've met several of them. I find them incredibly creepy and a little detached from reality for the most part.

You are famous for tracking down horror stars that rarely appear at conventions or have never done conventions before. Are they surprised by how strong their fandom is? How do they react to their first conventions?
I get a lot of "dead air" on the phone when I call them, that's for sure. The first show I ran myself was also the first ever *Dawn of the Dead* cast reunion ever held. I knew a few of the cast but found the rest of them with the help of my friend, Chris, by looking in a Pittsburgh phone book. (Remember phone books?) I had more than a few, "Who the hell are you and WHAT do you want to do?!" replies, but hooked them all the same and got most of the people contacted to join us.

With any first-time guest, once I get them to the show, they open up and start to have fun rather quickly. Most are truly amazed they have fans. Fortunately, until they meet up with the dread "guest rep" they are never greedy or charge more than their autographs will ever be worth. Once the "guest reps" get their claws into them, everything changes. Guaranteed.

You mentioned to me that fan conventions have changed a lot in the last 30 years, and not for the better. How have things gone downhill in your opinion?
Lack of organizational skills. An inability to multi-task or juggle all of the things you have to juggle if you are promoting a show. Cluelessness is a big factor. Cluelessness with a touch of greed is guaranteed to turn me off as a fan. There are just so many factors that go into running a fan show and it seems like very few promoters give them much thought these days.

I learned from the best. I learned how to run a show from real "show-men" like David Friedman, Ted V. Mikels, and Herschell Gordon Lewis - guys who knew how to get butts into seats when their movies weren't up to what theatre owners might call "Hollywood standards". These guys gave everyone a show to go along with their cheap films. Or, like Dave Friedman used to tell me all the time, "Sell them the sizzle, kid. Especially if the steak is a cheap cut of beef. They'll go away happy if you just give them a show." I've celebrated some of the worst "B" films ever released, but I had a great time doing it, and so did the fans who never thought they would see some-body celebrate a guilty pleasure "B" movie they always enjoyed.

Guests are also a factor in that I won't attend a convention as a fan any longer. Back in the 90s - ancient times I guess - guests would sign your stuff for free and usually had their own photos to sell for the whopping price of $5. Then, it got to be autographs were $5 across the board. No big deal. Five bucks is plenty worth getting something signed. But, in the space of ten years, things went from $5 to $10… $20… $30… $50 or more these days it seems. If I really want an autograph from somebody, I'll pay twenty bucks for it, but I'll get one, not have it personalized, and walk away. Charge less and I'll grab more than one. Charge more than twenty bucks, and I'll auto-matically walk away and not give you a second thought. Promoters can do a lot to keep autographs affordable, but few seem to give a shit. And it's the one thing I hear fans bitching about most these days.

And it seems the more a celebrity charges for his or her autograph, the shittier the actual signature is. For example, I don't think Norman Reedus is a very good actor. The guy can't even fake a Georgia accent, for cryin' out loud, but he's a nice enough guy, and back when he was $15 or $20 an autograph, I had a few friends who were *Boondock Saints* fans ask if I would get them an autograph if he was at a con I was at. If it wasn't any trouble, sure, I'd go up and get them one. And they all looked like an actual signature. Now the guy jerks off *Walking Dead* fans $80 or $100 a signature and it looks like a three-year-old made a squiggly line on paper and called it a "doggy" when they hand it to you. In the early 1990's I ran into Malcolm McDowell and asked him for a couple of autographs. They are beautiful signatures that you can read every letter of. And they were free. These days he charges, like, $50 for an autograph and it looks like an autistic kid drew you a mountain range. It's not a signature in any way, shape, or form, but people will line up to give the guy fifty bucks for whatever it is he scribbles and calls a signature. Why even do an appearance if you're going to care so little about your fans?

Don't even get me started on how much I hate "photo ops". You are paying money for something that has zero value and I will never offer them at my show. Buy an autograph or merchandise from a guest and get a free photo with your camera is how I like to work it. You can't ever sell an over-priced photo op photo. Nobody you know will ever want it when you're dead, and the person you just paid money to take a photo with doesn't even look like the person from the 25-year-old film you remember them from.

My solution is to just wander into any given old folks' home and take pictures with the residents. The old folks will appreciate the visit and you can tell people they are whoever you wish them to be. Who's going to know the difference? You can look cool to the people on your FB page that probably make fun of you behind your back anyway.

There are other things I don't like about the whole convention scene these days as a fan, but now I'm just depressing myself, so I'm going to go and have a drink...

Before you became a convention organizer you were a fan. Ever have any true fanboy moments encountering celebrities before you became one of their employers?

Sure. More times than I can count. I still have "fanboy" moments. You can't take the fanboy out of somebody just because they run their own convention. I run my show as a show I'd actually pay to attend myself as a fan.

I'll never forget meeting Peter Jackson in the hallway of a hotel in L.A. It was back before anybody but us fanboys knew who he was. *Meet the Feebles* just came out and it was only available in Japan. Me and my buddy Chris were standing there looking at a guy who looked familiar... He turns to me and says, "Doesn't that look like Peter Jackson, but fat?" He was slim in *Bad Taste*, so we knew what he looked like. We didn't know he ballooned up in the couple of years since *Bad Taste* came out, so we walked up to him and just said, "Peter Jackson?"... to which he replied, "Yes, how did you know who I am?" So we told him, "Hey, welcome to the world of fat guys!" since we certainly aren't small by anything except convention standards, and before you knew it, we were ushering him up to our room to have him sign some posters and stuff we bought just that day. Never did see him again all weekend. And yes, I still have all of the autographed stuff in my collection.

I bum rushed Vincent Price to say hello once in the 1980s and he held back his security guys telling them, "This boy is my fan. I wouldn't have a career without him." I used to write to him as a kid and just wanted to say hello in person.

Jack Nicholson gave me and my buddy an autograph on the hood of his limo while everyone behind us got cut off and pushed away.

I was one of the few people to make the show in NYC that Lucio Fulci attended. The blizzard of '95 it was. Anyway, it was the only U.S. appearance Fulci made before he passed away and I loved meeting that grumpy old bastard! I pestered him all weekend to the point that he started giving me a hard time on my way up to him, and I never knew if he was serious or just joking. I gave away a good 25 to 30 autographs to friends after that show because he signed everything I had, picked up at the show, and didn't sell on my table for me.

Keith Richards singled me out and gave me an autograph and some time after an Expensive Winos show once.

Me and a friend walked out of an elevator at the same time Christopher Lee walked out of another elevator on the same floor. He was in the States doing a book signing at a movie show and they kept him away from the fans unless he was signing or doing a predetermined talk. We say "hello" and my buddy tells him it's an honor to be one of the people who run his international fan club. Lee turns to him, asks his name, and proceeds to shoot the shit for twenty minutes with us in a hotel hallway. In all that time, one maid walked past us. She had no idea who he was. We didn't pester him for an autograph or piss him off in any way, shape, or form. We just shot the shit until it looked like his handler was getting nervous and let him go. It was fucking cool.

There are so many happy fanboy moments I have that didn't come from spending too much on an autograph or paying for some overpriced photo op. None of those would be happy memories in the least to me.

You have been interviewed many times. What are the funniest, strangest and most thought- provoking questions you have encountered?

Nothing is taboo or out of the ordinary for me to answer or talk about. Bring it on! Generally, people ask a lot of the same questions: What is my favorite movie? (I've watched way too many films to have just one favorite.) What made me want to start my own movie convention? (I wasn't having fun at them as a fan by the late 1990s and wanted to start one that I would actually attend if I weren't set up at it as a vendor.) I get a lot of the same old, same old.

Horror movies are an international phenomenon. Do you get many international fans at your shows, or fans of foreign horror movies?

Yes, and I'm extremely flattered. It seems the CW Show is internationally known and we had a big *Dawn of the Dead* fan fly in from Japan to attend our very first show. Since then, we've had fans from Ireland, Scotland, Australia, Germany, to name a few far-flung places I know of to fly in to enjoy what it is we do. Tons of fans come from Canada every show and that contingent seems to be growing every year. My wife does tickets and receipts, so she'd be the one to get a complete list from but she's always mentioning some new country to me. And I know that closer to home, we've had fans from damn near every state in the US attend the show.

Panels are a mainstay of conventions. Have you ever had one get out of hand? What happened? Which celebrities knew how to shut down hecklers?

I tend to host most every panel myself and I've never had one get out of hand. I've had some great panels though. Some that got ridiculously silly and some where the panel guests have gotten way too personal and maybe mentioned stuff they shouldn't have said to a crowd, but I can shut down a heckler in a heartbeat and love it when things get weird, so nothing is off limits and there is no direction I won't let a panel go.

Guest-wise, we get so many first-time guests or people who don't do a lot of convention appearances, so they seem to rely on me as the panel host to quell anything that may happen. But, there are some that handle a crowd very well. Fred "The Hammer" Williamson can tell his story better than anybody and keep a crowd hanging on his every word. Charles Band still gets nervous before doing his thing in front of a crowd, but settles in really quick and his inner "showman" comes out. And director Jeff Lieberman is a sarcastic bastard after my own heart and will shut somebody up in a heartbeat if need be.

Do fans ever confuse the actor with the characters they portray?
Yep. All the time. Just ask them. The stories they tell me are funny as hell sometimes. But, my personal favorite is when a fan doesn't believe that the person in front of them is actually the actor from the movie they know and love because the movie is 25 or 30 years old and the actors in the film get old and don't look like they did 25 or 30 years ago. Especially if they were in their 30s when they made the film. Now, all these years later, they are in their 60s or 70s and naturally look much older than they did.

What would your dream guest be in the future?
My dream guests are all dead now, so I'm going to go with the next person I find that hasn't done my show that fits what we celebrate. I've run 30 shows to date and have found new guests to invite every show. I've been able to bring in every mentor I ever wrote a letter to, talked to on the phone and/ or who gave me some advice in my younger days. But I celebrate films made from the late 50's through the end of the drive-in / beginning of the Mom and Pop video store days of the mid 1980's, so it's getting harder and harder to find new faces to invite and show a little Wasteland love to, so my dream is to just keep on finding new faces until I finally retire the show.

Have you ever had a celebrity make strange demands on you in order to be a guest at one of your shows?
Sure. I'm sure every promoter has. If it's within reason, I'm good. If it costs a bunch of money, is too demanding on me or my staff or requires more

attention that I give my wife, fuck off. End of conversation. No deal. Go away.

In an earlier question, I stated that a "no" is as good as a "yes" when inviting somebody to be a guest at the show and the real sin is not searching them out to invite them in the first place. Telling somebody to piss off after you talk to them has also happened once or twice. And I know from seeing certain guests at other cons that there are a few people I'd never in a million years even bother to invite to my show.

OK, now it's all you: What is the one knock-'em-dead, blow-their-socks-off fan convention story that you haven't told us yet? It can be funny, sad, scary, sexy, heart-warming, terrifying, sexy, action packed, cerebral, sexy or gross. Did I mention it could be sexy?

Other than the ones I've already mentioned...?

I don't mind telling anybody a story about my life on the road in person, but writing them down is a different animal altogether. If I avoid writing down a story that revolves around, and/or started or ends with massive amounts of alcohol, drugs, a hand gun, property damage, fire, or fleeing from the police, all the stories that fit into what you'd really like to hear are not printable as they actually happened. I can change the names to protect my "partners in crime" if you will but detailing a potential felony or possible unsolved crime is just not going to happen. How can anybody actually have a story that fits into what you ask that's wholesome? I'm no angel. I raised a lot of hell in my younger days and still manage to find myself ankle deep in shit from time to time, so I'm going to plead the 5th and go on to the next question...

What keeps you going, organizing two shows per year, year after year?

I'm a glutton for punishment.

I have been to conventions where there is one vendor who seems badly out of place, like they didn't know what kind of show they were buying a table at. Have you had any experiences like that?

Personally speaking, I like to be the odd man out so I've tried all kinds of shows I think may have some cross appeal over the years. I know what I'm getting into when I bought the tables or booth space, but choose to do the show just to see if being the odd man out will pay off.

I used to do a ton of comic book shows before there were more than 1,617 generic horror conventions running every weekend of the year, and I still do a couple of them every now and then. (What I won't EVER set up at is anything Wizard puts on.) I've done "paper and postcard shows", tattoo conventions, music related shows, toy and game shows, generic collectible shows, and model and modeling conventions over the years. Some worked out well while others not so much. But, if you don't attend them to see if there is any crossover interest in what you do and sell, you'll never know if it's an untapped source of paying the bills, right?

In closing, I'd like to tell anybody that may read this interview to never let anybody tell you "that won't work" or "how in the hell are you going to make a living doing that?" Life is short. Make the most of it. You may even become a jaded and crusty old "B"-Movie-lovin' hippie that somebody wants to interview every once in a while if you keep at it long enough.

Ryan Kopf

Ryan Kopf has been the chairman of more anime conventions than any other human. As the chief event organizer, <u>Ryan</u> spends a full-time 60+ hours per week organizing conventions. Usually, this time is spent between hand-designing and updating convention websites, emailing and calling staff and department heads, and reviewing convention rules and policies.

Can you give us a quick list of the fan conventions you have organized or attended?

AnimeCon.org organizes 8 annual anime conventions. So far, I think in total, I've been in charge of over 30? Maybe 50? Listing them all would be exhausting, so let's just mention the biggest two are AniMinneapolis and Anime Midwest. We're one of the biggest convention-running organizations around, and that's mostly because of our magic technology that helps automate con planning.

What is the strangest thing you have seen asked to be autographed?

I've seen all kinds of things autographed, but I'm not usually the one by the autograph booths. I've heard of program books, baseball cards, Yu-Gi-Oh cards, and even napkins getting autographed. Some attendees don't realize a guest will be there, and they grab anything they can think of because they don't want to miss out on their opportunity.

What is the sweetest or most touching thing a fan has said or done at one of your shows?

I've received some really sweet emails from attendees, telling us how either us (the conventions) or one of our guests has changed their life. We usually forward these onto all our staff to see as they're so heart warming.

You interact with fans and vendors at conventions. What is the strangest thing someone has tried to sell at one of your shows?

Nothing is strange to us. People sell all kinds of things.

Your show features voice actors, cosplayers, musicians and dancers. How do fans of different sub-genres interact with each other? Have you seen any funny or shocking confrontations between fans over the years?

The strangest con interactions are always with outside groups. People inside the convention are all nerds and they know what to expect. We even help build up to the con with emails about cosplay, events, con-going tips, et cetera. But people outside the con can either be really enjoyable or a real headache. We once had the convention at the same time as an Indian wedding. A real exotic affair. I heard a rumor there were elephants. They were some of the most pleasant people, they stopped to take dozens of photos, and they complimented everyone. But a few times we've been in the venue at the same time as a wedding, and the bride is always angry that someone is getting more attention than she. And everyone at a wedding is drunk. I don't like weddings overlapping cons.

What experiences have you had with fans who know far more about the celebrities of your various conventions than the celebrities themselves? How do various stars deal with that?

Every convention guest is different in the way they react to fans. Some absolutely love the attention and like to be rock stars. Some are a lot shyer, and ask, "Why am I so famous? How do you know so much about me? I don't even remember working on that show." It's funny to see the differences.

What is your average convention attendee like, and which person really surprised you by being a fan?

Our average attendee is amazing. Better than any other convention's attendee, and I'm being completely serious. Sometimes you'll go places and meet people who don't want to make friends, who just want to meet a guest and get out. Our attendees are all about the community, and every one of them wants to be part of something bigger than themselves. As for the most surprising fan, I lived in an apartment building a couple years ago and our neighbor was this really buff guy. But one day he heard about our anime conventions, and he wouldn't stop talking about *Bleach*. I was so surprised to find out how big of an otaku he was.

What other celebrity encounters have you had at conventions? Feel free to tell us any funny, sexy and/or terrifying close encounters you have had.

I'm so oblivious to who people are sometimes. The number of times I walk into a room and get introduced to people I never expected to meet is just too hard to count.

Have you ever been mistaken for someone else at a convention, and thought, "Why the Hell did you think I was them?" Have you had any celebrity guests mistaken for other people?

No, but many years ago someone said I looked like Orlando Bloom. I wish.

What is the one that got away? Which celebrity were you this close to getting only to have them pull out at the last nano second?

There are a few, but I can't go into personal details like that without their permission. Usually something like a wedding or family event comes up, and that tends to be a higher priority than a con.

Cosplay has become an art form. What costume at any convention has totally blown you away and amazed you with its high quality and detail? What is the all-time worst costume you have seen?

I can't pick one best costume. ;)

What super fans have you encountered whose whole lives have been consumed with one topic or movie they live for?

I don't think I know any that are obsessed with just "One Thing" (TM), but I know some superfans who don't want anything but reruns of *Doctor Who, Buffy,* and *Firefly.* They're usually super nice people, too; possibly influenced by those shows, haha!

What about stars who aren't convention regulars or are appearing at their first show? Are they surprised by how strong their fandom is? How do they react to their first conventions?

Some stars are completely surprised by how many fans they have. Others walk into a cheering room like a natural; smiles, waves, winks, you name it.

Fan conventions have gone from small gatherings to huge multi-media showcases. How has your show in particular changed and how has the type of celebrity who appears at them changed?

AnimeCon.org's conventions have always focused on our core, which has been our interactive, staff-lead events, such as the formal ball, date auction, and cosplay contest. The superstars are nice, and they bring in a lot of our attendees, but we have such an incredibly high attendee return rate because of our events. People come to AnimeCon.org conventions and make lifelong friends. We haven't changed from that core mission since year one. We also haven't changed from our principle of keeping autographs free. I don't like seeing people charged $25 for an autograph, because it leaves out some of the younger fans who just can't do that. We target that 16- to 24-year-old crowd, and we get them, and we make them the happiest.

Before you became a convention organizer you were a fan. Ever have any true fanboy moments encountering celebrities before you became one of their employers?

I've actually never been much of a fan of celebrities. At least not that I'll admit to, or show on the outside. ;) What hooked me on anime are the stories.

Photo ops are a convention favorite. Tell us about the more memorable ones you have seen.

So many people are posting pictures with Stan Lee, it's unreal.

Do you get many international fans at your shows, and how do they react to the North American version of anime and fandom?

We've gotten people from as far away as you can think of - China, Australia, and the Middle East. They all tell us how much they love our conventions, as they're so much more fan-focused and less corporate than other conventions.

Panels are a mainstay of conventions. Have you ever had one get out of hand? What happened? Which celebrities knew how to shut down hecklers?

The worst that might happen at an AnimeCon.org panel is some attendee thinking they are funnier than they are, and constantly interrupting with silly jokes. Occasionally we have to officially "shush" those types of hecklers.

Do fans ever confuse the actor with the characters they portray?

Fans often associate actors with their characters, yeah! And some actors ARE their characters. Greg Ayres is an amazing guy who plays a lot of loud-mouthed little kids; now he's just a loud-mouthed professional adult, haha! Most of our guests are their own characters. Some of our guests are so cool, that they're like caricatures of what a real person is like. YTCracker is like this super stealthy god-tier master computer cracker. DC Douglas is like the sexiest man alive. They're amazing.

What would your dream guest be in the future?

Dream guest... Johnny Depp, man. I want to drink rum with Johnny Depp.

Have you ever had a celebrity make strange demands on you in order to be a guest at one of your shows?

We've had a few interesting requests from our guests, but I don't think anyone has demanded anything like a "bowl full of green M&Ms". One of our guests this year is a bodybuilder and has QUITE the strict diet, and that's probably been our most in-depth request.

OK, now it's all you: What is the one knock-'em-dead, blow-their-socks-off fan convention story that you haven't told us yet? It can be funny, sad, scary, sexy, heart-warming, terrifying, sexy, action packed, cerebral, sexy or gross. Did I mention it could be sexy?

Knock 'em dead story? That's not even possible for me to answer because weird, amazing things are just a part of my life now. Guests dancing on stage in their underwear. Spontaneous swordfights or Nerf battles. Owl stuff. I can't even begin.

What keeps you going, organizing shows, year after year?

Running AnimeCon.org is the most fun job I could possibly have. I get to use my talents at computer programming to make it really (REALLY) easy, and then I get to have fun with other amazing people. Our staff team is so incredible that I couldn't imagine my life without them. My guests are often returning and are just dear friends to me. My whole life is cons and it's just lovely.

I have been to conventions where there is one vendor who seems badly out of place, like they didn't know what kind of show they were buying a table at. Have you had any experiences like that?

Hmmm, not that I can think of. We've had vendors who I thought wouldn't sell very well, like someone selling scented candles (not even anime themed) - yet they sold out! I'm just amazed.

Loren Lester

Loren Lester was an established face actor in such films as *Rock 'n' Roll High School* and TV series like *The Facts of Life* before he became the voice of Robin for an entire generation on *Batman: The Animated Series*, and proved to young viewers that kids could be more than mere sidekicks to adults in such classic episodes as "If You're So Smart, Why Aren't You Rich?," when Robin took the lead in the fight against the Riddler and Batman was shown to be one of the adults whose VCR was constantly flashing 12:00.

In addition to that iconic role, Loren's other superhero voices have included Green Lantern on *Batman: The Brave and the Bold*; Nightwing in several DC projects; Iron Fist in video games; Barbecue on *G.I. Joe*, and Flash Gordon's son in 66 episodes of *Defenders of the Earth*.

Amazingly, nobody ever thought to invite this pop culture legend to a fan convention as a guest until a couple of years ago, so if you haven't had a chance to meet him, he will hopefully be coming to a fan convention near you soon. He also continues to be a very busy actor in theatre, movies and voice acting.

Oh, and he was an attendee at the very first *Star Trek* convention, so it is official: he is cooler than you.

Can you give us a quick list of the fan conventions you have appeared at, as both a fan and celebrity guest?
I have only been doing this for about a year on the Wizardworld circuit, including the big show in Chicago. I love it.

What is the strangest thing you have been asked to autograph?
Tattoos. People will come to me with their tattoos of Batman and Robin and have me sign my autograph near the tattoos, and then they go to a tattoo artist who traces over my signature, turning it into a tattoo. There was also one convention that did a cast reunion of a movie I was in, *Rock and Roll High School*. A woman came up and wanted all six of us to sign her breasts.

What is the sweetest or most touching thing a fan has said or done for you?
I have been told repeatedly that when the show was originally aired, because it was before VCRs became more common, that the only way to watch the show was when it was being broadcast. Because we were on late in the afternoon, Batman was the first thing kids watched when they got home from school. I have been told by adults who were latchkey kids, raised by their grandparents or other relatives, kids who were bullied, et cetera, that we gave them a sense of empowerment, hope, and pleasure, and we were there for them every day. Now those fans have kids of their own who are the same age they were when the show was first on, and they can share the experience with them by watching it again. This has been going on for 30

years. Some of those fans have gone on to become animators, cartoonists and artists because of the show. One great artist, Kyle Higgins, told me he was inspired by the show and now creates his own stories. Some artists tell me that they hear my voice when they are drawing Robin or NIghtwing, and some people hear my voice when they read the comics. Lots of people who are amateur artists and fans of the show bring me fantastic depictions of Robin and Nightwing, including paintings and sculptures. One of them recently gave me a fantastic wire sculpture of Nightwing that is just beautiful.

Do fans ever get physical with you or invade your personal space?
No, and I've never been called on to fight like some action stars. One great reaction I do get is when I do the voice of Robin for young kids. Kids don't believe I'm Robin until they hear the voice. Then their faces light up.

You are most famous for your portrayal of Robin, a character that has been portrayed by many different actors. Do you ever appear at conventions with some of the other Robins?
No, but I would love to meet Burt Ward. That would be wonderful to do a convention with him. I did meet Casey Kasem once, and he was the very first actor to do the voice of Robin.

When I was at the Calgary comic book convention, a 400-pound guy stepped on my foot and I yelled out "Jesus Christ!" A cosplayer dressed as Jesus Christ (at least I think it was a cosplayer) promptly appeared and offered to heal me. What is your personal WTF story from any convention?
I don't have a story like that yet. But I have had people come up to me dressed in character and they refuse to break character. This happens especially with people dressed up like the Heath Ledger version of the Joker. Another time a lady came up dressed as Belle and she stayed in character the whole time. Harley Quinn is the most common character that women come dressed as, and that will get more so when the Harley Quinn movie comes out next year, and they all have big hammers. One guy came up to me and pulled out a gun. I knew it had to be fake because everyone is checked at the door for weapons, but I had a few brief seconds of shock before I remembered that.

What experiences have you had with fans who know far more about your characters than you could ever hope to know? How do you deal with that situation?

This happens to me every single time. People come up to me at conventions and they know the whole history of Robin and Nightwing in the DC universe. I can't keep up with all that, and I don't read comics, so that's how I keep track of how Dick Grayson is evolving.

What celebrity encounters have you had at conventions? Feel free to tell us any funny, sexy and/or terrifying close encounters you have had.

I have loved being at conventions with the Monkees, Peter Tork and Mickey Dolenz. At the St. Louis convention, Peter Tork got a hold of a Peter Tork mask, put it on, and then walked all around the convention floor imitating himself. It was a dream to meet Nichelle Nicholls and other members of the original *Star Trek* cast. She must be 80 but she is so beautiful, and very classy too. My daughter is a big fan of *The Walking Dead*, so I send her selfies of myself with cast members. I've had a lot of fun with Barry Bostwick, who has been going to conventions because of the 40th anniversary of *The Rocky Horror Picture Show*. He hosts the showing of the movie, and then does a little spiel about it and signs autographs, but he also entertains the really young kids at the conventions. He and I read them children's books, but he does a lot of commentary on the books, which is very funny for the adults too.

Have you ever been mistaken for someone else at a convention, and thought "why the Hell did you think I was them?"

At the last one I was at, two older guys, about 60 and dressed up as Batman and Superman, came up and one told the other that I was the original Robin. The other one started arguing and said I was too young to be Robin, because he thought that meant I was Burt Ward. Other people come up and ask if I was an artist on Batman, even though I am sitting under a huge sign that says I am a voice actor, but they see pictures from the show and assume I am a cartoonist. Sometimes I say yes I am the animator, but later on I say no.

There have been something like 40 different versions of Batman. Has anyone ever thought you were being disrespectful or blasphemous of the "true" Batman franchise?

No. Fans of Batman are fans of the show. People even say it is the best depiction of Batman they have ever seen, and there have been lots of movies and other stuff. For some people, Kevin Conroy is the ultimate Batman, I'm the ultimate Robin, and Mark Hamill is the ultimate Joker.

Cosplay has become an art form. What costume at any convention has totally blown you away and amazed you with its high quality and detail? What is the all-time worst costume you have seen?

I am blown away all the time. Some people are exact lookalikes of the celebrities they cosplay. I have met two exact lookalikes of Leonard Nimoy. Spock Vegas was one of them. Sometimes the costume is great, but the body doesn't quite match and you would never mistake them for the original, but sometimes you do. I met one guy who was an exact duplicate of Darryl from *The Walking Dead*, right down to every detail of his costume. He looked just like him. I have met lots of great Nightwings who look amazing. Sometimes the costumes are great but I have no idea who they are supposed to be. Luckily, I have a staff of people who follow me, manage me and explain who all the characters are.

You have been photographed thousands of times. What is your favorite photo with a fan?

I had my photo taken with a boy who was about 7 and who had made his own Nightwing costume, and it was fantastic. He said it was the highlight of his life to meet me. Of course, he hasn't been alive that long.

Gender bender cosplay continues to get more and more popular. Have you met a female version of one of your characters at conventions?

Definitely. One lady not only made her own Robin costume, but she makes aprons with Batman and Robin on them. I haven't seen a female Nightwing yet.

Before you became a celebrity you were a fan. Ever have any true fanboy moments encountering celebrities before you became one?

Before I started with Wizardworld, my only experience with comic book conventions was being a panelist at two of them, Comicon and Wondercon. I did attend the very first *Star Trek* convention, though. It was fantastic. The whole original cast was there and they all spoke. There were science fiction writers like Harlan Ellison and Anthony Burgess. Merchandising was not a big deal then, so there weren't a lot of vendors, but there were panels on things like whether space travel was possible and what its drawbacks would be. They had screenings of great movies like *A Boy and His Dog*. William Shatner spoke, and this was just after *Star Wars* came out, and whenever he said, "*Star Wars*," he said it with a real sneer. "Why did they make *Star Wars*? Why not *Star Trek*?" Of course, they started making *Star Trek* movies soon after.

You have been interviewed and done panels at conventions. What are the funniest, strangest and most thought-provoking questions you have encountered?

The thing I get asked over and over is why don't I do the voice of Robin all the time and in all the games. The thing people don't understand, and I don't blame them because they are not in show business, is that I have no control. I have to audition for roles. People don't understand that I got the role from auditions and not because I knew everything about the character. Only the biggest stars get to choose their roles. I just did the Batman/Harley Quinn animated movie, and it was the first time I have done Nightwing in a decade, but it wasn't by choice it was that long. When chosen to do it, I do it.

With your long list of credits, do fans ever want to discuss something with you that you have long forgotten?

No, but some of them do want to talk about older roles, like the ones I had on *Rock and Roll High School* or *The Facts of Life*. *Batman* fans do want to discuss every detail of every episode, though. If it's something I've researched or gone back and watched I'll know it, but otherwise, I won't.

You are constantly on the road. What is the hardest part about travel, and your funniest story from being on the road?

They take pretty good care of me, so it's not too bad. It can be hard being away, especially when I have an elderly mother and a dog, but it's usually only for a weekend. It's harder if it's two or three in a row. I love going to new places and walking around. Sometimes I get there a day early just so I can walk around. Doing this has given me a chance to visit places I've never been, like St. Louis, Nashville and Orlando.

Are kids ever amazed that you portray someone their age? What reaction do you get from young fans at shows?

When they realize I'm Robin, their mouth drops open, they go bug-eyed and they're stunned for a second, then they usually laugh. Sometimes they think it is so strange that they are a little scared, so it might be a nervous laugh.

Your voice is a big part of your career. At conventions, do you ever get so hoarse that you have to call it a day to save your voice?

No, I've been doing this for 40 years, so I know how to use my voice and not lose it. The only time I may get hoarse is if I'm doing voices in an interactive game which has lots of yelling and screaming.

OK, now it's all you: What is the one knock-'em-dead, blow-their-socks-off fan convention story that you haven't told us yet? It can be funny, sad, scary, sexy, heart-warming, terrifying, sexy, action packed, cerebral, sexy or gross. Did I mention it could be sexy?

One fan told me how he had lost his father as a child, and he came home to our show every day, and the empowering, positive message saved his life. He had been contemplating suicide. Our show got him through a rough time and now he has kids of his own. He told me this with tears in his eyes. It was incredibly touching.

LATCHKEY OF THE CHILDREN OF THE '90'S HAD NOTHING TO WORRY AOBUT THEM, BECAUSE THEY WENT HOME TO BATMAN AND ROBIN TO LOOK AFTER THEM.

APRIL FOOL'S DAY 2014: LOREN LESTER'S NEIGHBOR CALLS POLICE TO REPORT A ROBIN IN HER BIRDBATH

Mitch Markowitz

The birthdate of Mitch Markowitz is irrelevant. Birthdays are only useful in knowing how old a person was when they died, and he gained immortality in 1971 when the cult TV show *Hilarious House of Frightenstein* debuted. Mitch was the brother of producer Riff Markowitz and appeared in all 130 episodes and was there for the production of the whole show. Since then, he has been everything from the manager of world-famous magician Doug Henning to an actor to a real estate developer, and now is a frequent and popular guest at fan conventions, car shows and record stores. He is currently involved in trying to get the original *Frightenstein* back on the air, and to revive it with new episodes, and to create an animated adaptation.

Frightenstein, with its combination of short skits, bizarre characters, and cameos by the legendary Vincent Price, appealed to both kids and adults, as well as many local TV stations who were able to fill 130 hours of programming time with one purchase. The show has been seen around the world and has been released on DVD. If you don't know what it is, quickly watch an episode on You Tube and then come back to this book. You'll be glad you did.

Can you give us a quick list of the fan conventions you have appeared at, as both a fan and celebrity guest?

I've done Fan Expo Canada many times, as well as comicons in Niagara Falls, London, Oshawa, Hamilton, Burlington, and Kitchener. In Kitchener,

I was the Grandmaster of their Zombie Walk. I've also done the horror con, Shock Stock, in London, and the Carnival of ParaHorror in Buffalo. I've also done lots of car shows.

What is the strangest thing you have been asked to autograph?

Body parts. Everyone you can name. Also tattoos, usually of characters from the show. The fans with tattoos are usually at the car shows. I don't charge for autographs. I make enough from the promoters. I hand out my autographed posters and make a point of talking to every fan. I like to learn about them and where they watched the show. I met one lady who watched it with her parents in Madrid, Spain. I was headlining the Motorama Show in Toronto and this guy came up with his lovely red-headed wife. He turned out to be the head of the animation school in Oakville. I told him there was a documentary in the works about *Frightenstein* and asked if he was interested in doing some animation for it. He was thrilled, and I set up a meeting for him with the producers to do some Disney-style animation. If I had just signed him an autograph and moved on to the next person, that would never have happened.

What is the most inappropriate thing a fan has done or said to you? What about the flipside? What is the sweetest or most touching thing a fan has said or done for you?

The most inappropriate was also the sweetest. A lady came up and she began crying uncontrollably. I had never seen anything like it. I had to go in front of the table and hug her and calm her down. I have never had a reaction like that and wasn't expecting it. She just got so emotional she couldn't control herself.

Have you had people come up to you dressed as one of your characters?

Many times, usually the Count or Igor, or the Wolfman. I am amazed at the energy people put into their costumes and the detail they put in. I've seen a couple of Griseldas and one Dr. Pet Vet. He was great. He told me how much he hated that goddamned sloth when he was a kid because he wouldn't let Igor have a pet.

When I was at the Calgary comic book convention, a 400 pound guy stepped on my foot and I yelled out "Jesus Christ!" A cosplayer dressed as Jesus Christ

(at least I think it was a cosplayer) promptly appeared and offered to heal me. What is your personal WTF story from any convention?

Shock Stock flipped me out. There was a Miss Shock Stock contest, and I only learned after the fact that the contestants were porn stars. The after-party was in the same hotel as the show, and most of the guests and attendees stayed there. The action went on all night. Then there was a film festival, and I didn't realize they were showing *Human Cattle*, a short I was in. The next day, there was an awards ceremony, and I won for best short and best special effects. They didn't give me any advance warning, so I was totally surprised.

The environment of the whole show in Buffalo was weird. It was a combination paranormal and horror show, held in this abandoned train station that had been closed for years. They took me on a tour of it and it was really spooky. It was a 25-story building that looked like one big haunted house. There was dust and abandoned property everywhere. The vendors were all horror or paranormal related too.

Are people surprised to meet you? Do they expect you to be one thing but not the others?

My whole presence surprises them. I am best known for *Frightenstein*, but I was almost unrecognizable on screen as Super-Hippie because I wore a big blonde afro wig and fake sideburns. People see my poster, and then they all do the same thing. They take a couple of steps and say, "Oh my God! I watched that show as a kid!" Then they come back and we have a good talk. Everybody knows Hasselhoff or Shatner instantly, but it is fun to see them have that moment of realization when they figure out who I am. There was one guy at the last show in London who had read about the show ahead of time and came to see me even though Shatner was the big draw.

I had a chance to talk to Shatner at that show. In the 1970s, my Brother Riff produced a game show called *Party Show*. Billy Van and Dinah Christie were regulars, and Shatner was often a guest star. It was two teams of celebrities doing charades. He remembered it and we had a good talk for five or ten minutes, but he never once looked at me. He kept signing autographs the whole time. He probably made $4000 while talking to me.

What experiences have you had with fans who know far more about you than you could expect them to know? How do you deal with that situation?

Everybody knows more than I do. Everyone I meet at these shows is a true fan. 90% are what I call purists. They know every detail of the show. I was doing one panel discussion with about 150 people and was about five or ten minutes into it when this lady asked some question about some minute detail in one episode, and I was dumbfounded. I just looked at her and said, "Why are you such a fucking nitpicker?" The next question was the same thing, and I asked the guy, "Are you with the fucking FBI? Have you spent the last 45 years taking notes for this moment?" Unbeknownst to me, somebody had their camera phone on, and you can find it on You Tube if you search "fucking nitpicker".

What other celebrity encounters have you had at conventions? Feel free to tell us any funny, sexy and/or terrifying close encounters you have had.
I've had lots of them. At Shock Stock, I met Felicia Rose for the first time. She does the *Sleepaway Camp* movies. The promoter introduced us, and I always stand out as the best- dressed guy at the conventions because everyone else is in a black tee-shirt and jeans. We were really taken with each other. She is amazing, very beautiful and talented. We have kept in touch because she wants us to work together sometime. I also met Alice Cooper at Fan Expo. He is a great guy. He is a huge fan of the show. I'm working on a reboot of the show, with Alice Cooper doing the Vincent Price introductions, and Felicia Rose doing Griselda. They are both into it.

I used to manage bands in the 60s, and there was one band that broke us. The guy who played bass and drums, Whitey Grant, went on to play with Alice, and later Lou Reed. Alice remembered him, and said he was a small, slight guy but was the only one he ever met who could drink Alice under the table.

I am always busy at shows, but not as much as the big names. I was beside Robert Englund at one show. My line-up was usually six to twenty people and his was usually 300. Then, I was working away and looked up, and I suddenly had over 100 people in line. It turned out that Alice had just done a panel and said *Frightenstein* was his all-time favorite show and that everyone should go talk to me about it.

Another time I was at a show and all of the celebrities were sitting at the same long table. I went over to introduce myself to the guy closest to me, who was about six feet away. I hadn't seen him come in. It was Dean

Yauger, and he stood up, and up and up. He's a big guy, and I'm only about 5'9". Then he introduced me to the guy who sat beside him, and he was even bigger. He had played Leatherface in *The Texas Chainsaw Massacre*. He had no idea who I was. His face was just blank, like a deer in the headlights. I asked him where he grew up, and he said Ohio. I knew the show was shown there, so I showed him a poster. He pointed at the librarian, and asked if that guy fell asleep a lot. I said that was him. Then he pointed at Griselda and asked if she always banged her head on a pot. I said yes. Then we had a great time.

I did a panel with Lisa Loring once. She is great. Everyone wants to ask her questions about *The Addams Family*, but she was so young when she did that, she has no memories. She told me to do all the talking, and we had a great time. I've also done interviews with Victoria Price. The problem is her dad was constantly on the road, and he never even told her he spent four days once doing all the segment intros for my show. I gave her a few anecdotes that she could tell the interviewer. Vincent was a great guy. So classy and elegant. She is the same way.

I've met lots of musicians who have used video clips from the show. One guy had played with two Juno-winning bands and started his own band, Spinning Rose. He asked for my blessing to use clips of Wolfman and Super-Hippie in a video for his song, Spinning Rose. I said yes and also did the intro and outro for the video. You can see it on You Tube. There's even a band in Calgary called Frightenstein, but I've never had contact with them.

He wasn't a celebrity, but one funny encounter at a show was with a cop from New York. He credited the show with slowing down the drug trade every day from 3:30-4:30 because all of the dealers ran home to watch it. I was glad to do my part.

My funniest non-contact with a celebrity was one year at Fan Expo. It used to always be the last weekend in August, so I got dressed up and went to the convention hall. The back wasn't open like it normally was, so I tried the front. There were usually a couple of hundred guys waiting to be the first ones in, but this time there was nobody. Finally, some people come by, but they're all headed to a Blue Jays game. Finally, I called my wife, and she checked the calendar, and they had moved the show to Labour Day weekend... I have a great photo of me yelling "HOLY SHIT!" over my stupid mistake.

Have you ever been mistaken for someone else at a convention, and thought "why the Hell did you think I was them?"

Not at shows, but I have often been mistaken for Paul Anka. I don't see it. We're both kind of swarthy, and were both Jewish guys from Ottawa, but that's about it. I was in a restaurant after a show in Florida, and a drunk lady came up to me asking if I was Paul Anka. I said no, but she didn't believe me. She figured I was really Paul Anka and didn't want to be noticed. Naturally, she told everyone in the restaurant and pretty soon everyone was staring at me.

Amazingly, there are two Mitch Markowitzes in the entertainment world. One of them is me, and the other wrote *Good Morning Viet Nam*. I never correct people, but the other one probably does.

Cosplay has become an art form. What costume at any convention has totally blown you away and amazed you with its high quality and detail? What is the all-time worst costume you have seen?

The best ones are usually Harley Quinn. There are lots of them, and they all put lots of effort into the character. The worst ones are the ones who put no effort into it and just want to play for a weekend.

You have been photographed thousands of times. What is your favorite photo with a fan, and what was the one request that made you shake your head, laugh or throw up a little in your mouth?

My favorite one was a lady who was maybe 25 and at the show with her parents. She pulled up her dress for the photo and showed this great tattoo on her leg of Vincent Price and told me she was getting my face put on her other leg for next year. I said I had no problem with being photographed with her tattoos as long as she wasn't wanted by the police.

I also love the photos where there are three generations of a family who watch the show. The grandparents saw the first run, the kids watched the reruns, and the grandkids see it online or on DVD. The grandparents are so happy to show them what they watched as a kid.

The worst ones are the ones who pick me up. It happens every show. Sometimes they don't even realize they do it. They hug me and lift me up because they are so enthusiastic. They never give any warning.

Gender bender cosplay continues to get more and more popular. Have you met a male version of your character at conventions? What was that like?

Our characters all wore heavy makeup. Remember, Griselda was actually a guy. So, I don't know they're doing gender bender until they talk to me. I've met female counts and a male Griselda. I love cosplayers.

Before you became a celebrity you were a fan. Ever have any true fangirl moments encountering celebrities before you became one?

Before I did shows, I was always awestruck when I met someone. I met Shelly Berman when he was really big, and he and Bob Newhart were the two guys with the biggest selling comedy albums. Now he plays Larry David's dad on *Curb Your Enthusiasm.*

I used to tour with the magician Doug Henning. This was before he was a world-famous magician. He was also a mime, and we toured for the Shoe Agency of Canada, a government office. He did mime and magic, and we toured shopping tours everywhere.

Actually, I still get awestruck. It just wears off quicker than it used to. I hope I never stop being awestruck. My wife gets that way too. At one show she got to meet Pat Mastroianni from the *Degrassi* series. She grew up in the States, but she saw the show. She was in heaven. I got her a poster of him to put on her closet door so she can see him every morning. Steve Kerzner is on her other closet door. He did Ed the Sock. He's a great guy with a very caustic sense of humour.

Have you been interviewed and done panels at conventions? What are the funniest, strangest and most thought-provoking questions you have encountered?

The strangest are the ones that read way too much into the show. The show was designed to be intellectually accessible to five-year-olds. It is hard to write jokes for kids that age, so we used sight gags. We took the biggest guy we could find and had him play Igor, and the smallest guy we could find, Guy Big, and teamed them up. There is something funny about that. Lots of people didn't know what to make of the show. When Westinghouse syndicated the show to a Los Angeles station, the suits had no idea what the show was. They put us on 11:30 to 12:30 at night, opposite Johnny Carson. Carson was this tight-assed Midwestern conservative. He cringed when guys like Tiny Tim were on the show. California has the most college students of any state, and by 11:30 the kids were done studying and smoking a doobie. They preferred us to Carson, and we beat him in the ratings. I even have a TV Guide advertising us in LA. We followed the Marx Brothers. It wasn't what we were about, but that's what people read into it. The show was completely innocent. When we sold the show in the beginning to CHCH, they provided the hard costs, like cameras and production facilities. We provided the soft costs like sets and scripts. Instead of getting real writers form New York or somewhere, we went to Ryerson, which was a trade school in those days, and asked their TV arts program for their ten best students. I think we paid them $12 a week each, but they were thrilled. There was nothing deep in our show, but everyone was trying to read these "Paul is dead" conspiracies into it. Why discourage them if they were watching? I just play along with that stuff, like the internet rumor that I was the mosquito on the show. It was actually Billy Van, but if IMDb wants to give me the credit, why not?

Have you done any foreign conventions yet? What was that like?
Not yet, but I am this close to protecting *Frightenstein* as a brand. The show would go back into reruns, there would be a reboot, and an animated version. Then we'd have a shot at getting worldwide attention. I would love to have someone like Eugene Levy to play the professor. Someone did a *Frightenstein* album recently, and it sold out.

You are constantly on the road. What is the hardest part about travel, and your funniest story from being on the road?
The hardest part is being away from your wife and family. My son is 28 now and is on the road a lot himself now. It's tough. It makes a lot of people turn to drugs or alcohol or sleeping around. Being on the road is not an excuse for that kind of behavior, but people don't know what else to do. In *The Last Waltz*, Martin Scorsese asks Robbie Robertson why he would quit after 16 years on the road, and he said it was because he had spent 16 years on the road, and it was a goddamned miserable life. When I was managing bands, I had one lead guitarist who never drank or anything like that. Every town we were in, he'd go to a museum or do something cultural. Most people would rather drink all night. There was one time the band I was road-managing got a five-night gig in a bar. That was rare, because there were more venues in those days, from clubs to high school dances. Now everyone gets DJs. Anyway, we got put up in a hotel. I slept on a rollaway cot. I fell asleep

in my underwear. I was so thin in those days, the guys folded up the bed with me in it and latched the top. I have no idea how I ended up by the main desk in the lobby. At least I hope I was wearing underwear, because someone finally let me out. I thought I was up shit creek that time.

OK, now it's all you: What is the one knock-'em-dead, blow-their-socks-off fan convention story that you haven't told us yet? It can be funny, sad, scary, sexy, heart-warming, terrifying, sexy, action packed, cerebral, sexy or gross. Did I mention it could be sexy?

Shock Stock. Like I said, I didn't know the people there. I got to talking with this girl Samantha Mack. Nice lady. Beautiful face, nice figure. She is really funny and smart, so I decided to look up her Twitter feed. It was only when I started reading about 20 new positions to have sex in that I realized she is a major porn star. She is really sweet though. I just normally don't read about that, and my face showed it.

The other one is when my son went to university. I hate to fly, so I was hoping for a school in Ontario. Instead, he picks University of Victoria in BC. I thought holy fuck, a massive plane ride. But they gave him a 50% scholarship, so we went out there with him, got him settled in a dorm. I showed him around because I had been there lots of times with bands. He called me the next day. He is a really conservative guy. I'm not sure how that happened when my wife and I are so liberal about everything. Anyway, he wandered down to the student lounge and people were watching *Frightenstein*. I came on the screen as Super-Hippie, and without thinking, he said I was his dad. He normally doesn't talk about that. Suddenly, he was famous on campus as Son of Super-Hippie. It wasn't the image he was going for.

Vic Mignogna

If you don't know who Vic Mignogna is, you probably think that "anime" is the name of a waitress at your local Hooters.

He has more than 250 IMDb credits, almost all of them as a voice actor in the most beloved anime franchises of all time. In addition to his most famous role in *Fullmetal Alchemist*, he has worked on *Bleach, One Piece, Pokemon, Digimon, RWBY, Dragonball, Dragonball Z* and *Naruto*.

As a singer, his various songs on You Tube have combined views of more than 5 million. Most of his songs have an anime connection.

As a face actor, he is most famous for his many roles in various fan productions set in the *Star Trek* Universe, most notably as Captain Kirk. He has also appeared in fan productions devoted to *Futurama* and *Doctor Who*.

He also has IMDb credits for music department, as a composer, director, producer, writer, assistant director, set decorator, editor and the guy who does whatever nobody else wants to do.

As a convention guest, he is in constant demand around the world. His panels are a combination of comedy, live music, Q and A and personal stories about his many years in the business.

Despite his busy schedule, Vic was one of the first celebrities who volunteered to take part in this book. He values his fans and his connection with them.

Can you give us a quick list of the fan conventions you have appeared at, as both a fan and celebrity guest?
I used to attend conventions as a fan when I was a little boy, primarily *Star Trek* conventions and then a couple *Star Wars* conventions. But in my 20 years as a voice actor I have been a guest at several hundred conventions around the world... Too many to list!,

What is the strangest thing you have been asked to autograph?
I've been asked to sign a lot of interesting items, but perhaps some of the most unique are peoples' inhalers, and even someone's car! I've also been asked to sign several peoples' bodies, that they then had the signature tattooed!

What is the most inappropriate thing a fan has done or said to you?
I really haven't had many inappropriate questions or requests from fans. I've been quite lucky in that regard! But I would probably say that a fan requesting me to let her lick my hand, a fan giving me an envelope with a lock of her hair in it are among the top :-)

What about the flipside? What is the sweetest or most touching thing a fan has said or done for you?

I hate to sound like a broken record, but there are way too many wonderful, kind and endearing interactions over the years. I don't think I could list just one for fear of it diminishing the hundreds of others. But suffice to say my fans have blessed me with their kindness and support for more than I deserve over the years.

Do fans ever get physical with you or invade your personal space?

My fans have always been very respectful. I think they know that I love and respect them and they treat me in kind. Fans always request hugs, but I am honored to oblige them. If I can bring a little light into their lives, I'm happy to do so. Perhaps my favorite part about my interaction with the fans is the privilege to encourage them or help them through difficult times in their lives.

You have portrayed Captain Kirk in fan productions of Star Trek. How do other fans react to your portrayal of such an iconic figure?

The fan response to *Star Trek Continues* has been overwhelming. It has surpassed my wildest expectations! Not only do hard-core *Star Trek* fans enjoy our series, but we've actually brought a lot of new fans to *Star Trek,* especially anime fans familiar only with my voice work.

When I was at the Calgary comic book convention, a 400 pound guy stepped on my foot and I yelled out "Jesus Christ!" A cosplayer dressed as Jesus Christ (at least I think it was a cosplayer) promptly appeared and offered to heal me. What is your personal WTF story from any convention?

And one such moment for me was when fans began cosplaying as me! Not a character I played... ME!

What experiences have you had with fans who know far more about your characters than you could ever hope to know? How do you deal with that situation?

I'm always very grateful when fans tell me more about my character that I knew! When you work on several shows at the same time, you often don't have a chance to do a great deal of research on any one character. Some of my favorite lines of characters I've played come from fans sharing their favorite lines.

Your convention appearances include singing and you generally go way out of your way to entertain your fans. How draining is that?

It actually takes a lot more energy to interact enthusiastically with hundreds of people a day than you would think! But as I said before, I am so deeply grateful to God for the privilege to do what I do, that I am more than happy to expend every ounce of energy I have to make sure the fans have a great and positive experience.

What celebrity encounters have you had at conventions? Feel free to tell us any funny, sexy and/or terrifying close encounters you have had.

One of the many blessings of getting to be a guest at pop culture conventions is the chance to meet some of my childhood heroes. It has been so surreal and crazy cool to actually become friends with people like William Shatner, Lou Ferrigno, Henry Winkler, Michael Dorn, Marina Sirtis, and many others... people whose work I loved when I was younger.

Have you ever been mistaken for someone else at a convention, and thought "why the Hell did you think I was them?"

Early on in my voice acting career I was mistaken at a few conventions for another voice actor from Canada named Scott McNeil. He's a very talented prolific voice actor for many years, and we have a similar physical appearance. Once I even dressed up as him at a convention he was at!

For some people, Star Trek isn't entertainment; it's a religion. Has anyone ever thought you were being disrespectful or blasphemous of the "true" Star Trek?

Absolutely not. Everyone who has seen our work knows that we want only to pay tribute and homage to a show that meant a great deal to us.

Cosplay has become an art form. What costume at any convention has totally blown you away and amazed you with its high quality and detail? What is the all-time worst costume you have seen?

I am regularly blown away by the amazing costumes I see at conventions. When I was younger, I used to build props and costumes myself, so I have great appreciation for the talent that goes into these things.

You have been photographed thousands of times. What is your favorite photo with a fan, and what was the one request that made you shake your head, laugh or throw up a little in your mouth?

There've been a few times people have asked me to flip the bird with them to a friend of theirs. I'm not usually comfortable with something like that, but I have, on occasion, done it because I knew it would please the fan if I did :-)

I have also been asked many times to sign girls' breasts. That's something I'm not comfortable with and I do my best to graciously decline.

You are one of the hardest working celebrities on the convention circuit in terms of the amount you travel and the number of shows you do. What response have you gotten in other countries? How do Japanese people react to your portrayal of Japanese characters?

I have always been blown away by the kind and enthusiastic response I get in other countries. Even today it's humbling and a bit overwhelming to think that people in other countries are familiar with my work and enjoy it. Getting fan letters from places like Iran, Egypt, Russia is always a thrill. I was even surprised when I visited Japan at the response I got, even though they are not generally familiar with the English voice actors.

Gender bender cosplay continues to get more and more popular. Have you met a female version of one of your characters at conventions? What was that like?

Yes, I have met some gender bender versions of some of my characters. I think it's cool! I always applaud and support anyone's expression of their creativity.

Before you became a celebrity you were a fan. Ever have any true fanboy moments encountering celebrities before you became one?

I'll never forget when I got to meet Leonard Nimoy. He was speaking at a college nearby, and it was not a standard convention setting. But I found out about it and went to the college, even though I was only about 13 years old.

Full Metal Alchemist is an incredibly popular franchise with intensely loyal fans. How do they compare to Trekkies?

It is such a privilege to be a part of such an amazing series like *Full Metal Alchemist*. It certainly has a big and loyal fan base, and I'm honored to be a part of it!

Star Trek had its 50th anniversary. Did you take part in the celebrations at all?
I celebrated the 50th anniversary of *Star Trek* by attending the big *Star Trek* convention in Vegas!

Your voice is a big part of your career. At conventions, do you ever get so hoarse that you have to call it a day to save your voice?
Yes, my voice is extremely important to me both as a voice actor and singer, and I tend to abuse it a lot! I always have to be careful at conventions that I don't overdo it, since I usually have to record the following week!

That's all I have time for! So let me just finish by saying I am so grateful to God for the privilege to do what I do, and I will never cease to be amazed and humbled by the fans and their enthusiasm. I hope I can continue to do what I'm doing now for many years to come!

Nathan O'Brien

In 2006 Nathan moved to Spokane from Whidbey Island, WA. Since then he's made it his goal to bring a slice of the comic book and pop culture world to the Inland Northwest. As a freelance artist it's also been a personal goal of his to support local businesses and provide an affordable event for all ages.

Can you give us your name, and a quick list of the fan conventions you have organized or appeared at, as both a fan and attendee?

I am the founder of the Lilac City Comicon, which is in its 12th year in Spokane, WA. Before that, I took part in the Emerald City Comiccon as an artist in their Artist Alley. As a fan, I've been to shows in Rose City, Tacoma, and several times to San Diego.

What is the strangest thing you have seen asked to be autographed?

People want sketches done on their body. As an artist, I wouldn't do that. If they want to turn their idea into a tattoo, then I'll do a sketch and they can take that to a tattoo artist.

What is the most inappropriate thing a fan has done or said at one of your conventions? What about by a celebrity guest?

Guests are pretty good. One time when I was in the Emerald City Artist Alley, there was a professional artist two tables down from me who was having a bad day. His original flight was cancelled and his luggage was lost, so he missed the whole first day of the show. When he finally got to his table, he just said "F this!", put his boots on the table, pulled out a bottle of whiskey and started doing shots. He ended up getting kicked out.

What about the flipside? What is the sweetest or most touching thing a fan has said or done at one of your shows?

There are different examples every year. Guests love interacting with their fans. Two years ago, I had Steve Cardenas, who played the red Power Ranger, Rocky. He did a panel and a Q and A. There was a little boy who was five or six in a red Power Ranger suit, and he went up to the mike and just said he wanted to meet Steve. Steve told him to come up on stage and gave him a big hug and took a picture with him. There were about 250 people watching and it was great.

What is the strangest thing a vendor has tried to sell at your shows?

I have very strict policies on what vendors can sell. If there's nudity in an artist's work, it is not displayed to the public. If they want to have it off to the side in a binder or something, fine. One year I had a guy selling Bettie Page-style pinup art, and there was nudity in everything he sold. I made him put Post-It notes on the inappropriate parts. He wasn't happy, but he had signed a contract.

Your different shows appeal to different subgenres. How are the fans different?

They really aren't different from each other, other than the fact that Spokane has lots of *Dr. Who* fans for some reason, so that draws lots of *Dr. Who* vendors. Everyone comes for their own reasons.

When I was at the Calgary comic book convention, a 400 pound guy stepped on my foot and I yelled out "Jesus Christ!" A cosplayer dressed as Jesus Christ (at least I think it was a cosplayer) promptly appeared and offered to heal me. What is your personal WTF story from any convention?

One memory that stands out is that one year there was a celebrity guest who was late. I couldn't figure it out because I knew they had arrived in town the day before. They finally came in and said, "OK, let's get this over with" and handed me their dog, with instructions on when to feed it, give it water, take it outside, everything. I ended up being a dog-sitter all day.

What experiences have you had with fans who know far more about the themes of your various conventions than you would expect them to know? How do you deal with that situation?

This happened just last year. Tim Russ was in *Star Trek: Voyager*, and he is super polite and professional, but the series was a few years ago and he doesn't remember everything from every episode, while *Star Trek* fans remember every detail possible. I had my friend Jesse, who is a *Star Trek* super-fan, sit with Tim, and he was supposed to be there to keep the line moving and deal with people, but afterwards Tim thanked me for Jesse because he could answer all the questions about minute details that Tim had forgotten about.

What is your average convention attendee like, and which person really surprised you by being a fan?

The most popular costumes are anything *Dr. Who*-related, plus Harley Quinn and Deadpool. 40% of the attendees are female. The age range is usually 18 to early 30s. We get lots of families. At the door, we charge $5 less for families to encourage them to come. I can't think of any unusual attendees.

What about haters? Have people come to your conventions just to say how much they hate horror or your particular guests?

There are always some. When you're putting on a pop culture event, you have to make sure that different movies, TV shows and fiction are represented. I am constantly asked why I don't bring in pro wrestlers. My take on it is that I liked wrestling as a kid, but all of the wrestlers I liked are probably dead now or living in Atlanta, which is where the TNT wrestling program originated. I'm not going to pay to fly someone across the country. I'm just not into it. One year a guy asked me why there were no wrestlers, and I said because I wasn't interested, and he really took it the wrong way. He said, "What do you mean what I want doesn't matter? Are you saying the fans don't matter?" I just meant it wasn't something I'm interested in.

I bring in lots of *Power Rangers* guests. It was a show I loved as a kid and it's still going strong. They draw really well, but some attendees complain about it. "Oh, God! Not another Power Ranger!"

What other celebrity encounters have you had at conventions? Feel free to tell us any funny, sexy and/or terrifying close encounters you have had.
San Diego is a real Hollywood-type show, so you run into celebrities whether you're at panels, on the floor or outside the building. One year, Elijah Wood was five feet away from me, just on his own and waiting to cross the street. Another year I was in the restroom, and the Undertaker from the WWF was using the urinal beside me, and he's like seven feet tall.

There were a couple of years that I went to San Diego with some friends of mine and we'd go to a little out-of-the-way coffee shop in the morning rather than get coffee at the show. This way, we got in and out fast. One time, as we were going in, Nathan Fillion came out with his hands full with three or four coffees. My friend yelled, "Nathan! High five" and Fillion ducked him, yelling, "Don't touch me!" That became a joke among my friends for years, with people yelling, "Don't touch me!" when someone wanted a high five.

Have you had any celebrity guests mistaken for other people? How about yourself?
I haven't been mistaken for anyone, but one of my volunteers, Richard, kind of looks like me even though he's ten years younger, and celebrities and vendors are always confusing him for me.

My mom comes to the show sometimes because she likes to feel included. Sometimes she'll go up to a guest and say how much she likes their movies, and it will be a comic book artist.

What is the one that got away? Which celebrity were you this close to getting only to have them pull out at the last nano second?

Once it was Doug Jones. I had him booked for a year. I was really excited about him because I had heard nothing but good things about him. A friend of mine had run into him at an after-party of a different show and asked him if it was true he was a contortionist. He was sitting at a really high table, and from a sitting position he swung one of his legs up on it and asked, "What do you think?" I had wanted him for 3 or 4 years and the show was finally big enough to afford him. I had even purchased his plane ticket, and then 6 or 7 weeks before the show a conflict with filming popped up. I had already been advertising him as a guest for months.

Cosplay has become an art form. What costume at any convention has totally blown you away and amazed you with its high quality and detail? What is the all-time worst costume you have seen?

We have some very talented people. Spokane is a border town with Washington and Idaho, and we are a long way from Seattle and Boise, so we are the only show a lot of people go to. We are their San Diego. There is one lady who has developed a real following. She lives on her own in a studio apartment and she spends all year working on her costume. She only stands about 5 feet tall, and last year she came as a 7 foot tall Groot. She was on stilts and her costume was covered with wood and bark. She even had a voice modulator to sound like him. She couldn't take two steps without someone wanting to take a picture with her.

What super fans have you encountered whose whole lives have been consumed with one topic or movie they live for?

There are attendees who come for one thing and that's it. The thing is, if they have to pay admission and then a high autograph or photo op fee, they aren't going to spend money on anything else. A few years ago, there was another convention in town, but they were one and done. They brought in Shatner and Stan Lee, both of whom have huge guarantees. At this point in time, they were tied for being the number one draw on the convention circuit. The vendors were furious because they sold nothing. People came for Lee or Shatner and then left.

How do stars react to their first conventions?

Positively. They are usually overwhelmed in a good way. We are the only show in the vicinity, so the fans treat them great. We also have about 50%

cosplayers, so there is great star/attendee interaction, especially the ones for whom it is a first or second show.

How have conventions changed over the years?

The shows have evolved to be more like the San Diego model. They are very celebrity-focused. I tried to keep out of that for the first nine years, but we moved into a bigger venue and we need them to draw fans. The show has to stay relevant. People look forward to it.

The other big change has been security. There has been a heightened awareness for the need to keep fans safe. The focus used to be on catching scalpers or people reusing someone else's pass. Now the focus is on keeping weapons out and protecting cosplayers. One year at the Phoenix con, they caught a guy dressed as the Punisher who had real firearms. He admitted that he was there to kill Jason Frank, who played the Green Power Ranger. This all happened about a week before my show. I knew I had to do something in response because it is a thousand times worse if you do nothing and an incident does happen. We brought in metal detectors, and some people were up in arms about it. It started a huge debate on gun control. But, as conventions grow, they have to be treated the same as sporting events or concerts. These changes are here to stay. I will never apologize for making things safe for people.

Before you became a convention organizer you were a fan. Ever have any true fanboy moments encountering celebrities before you became one of their employers?

There is an old saying that you should never meet your idols, but there have been moments when I have met people I admired and not regretted it. One year in San Diego, I went to the Brian Singer panel about *Superman Returns*. I sat in the back by the door because I was a little late. At the end of the panel, they said Singer was going to be taken immediately to the WB booth. So they took him out one door and I was the first guy out the other door, and I ran right into him. I asked him to sign my bracelet. He started to make an X and joked that he was still thinking X-Men and not Superman. He turned the X into an S and signed it. I told him how much I loved *The Usual Suspects*. Then I looked up and realized we were surrounded by about 200 people, all of them trying to get to him while security tried to hustle him to the booth.

Panels are a mainstay of conventions. What is your most memorable one?

As my show grows, I have less time to watch panels. I used to moderate some of them. The most memorable panel I ever saw was in San Diego for *Through a Scanner Darkly*, the movie based on the Philip K. Dick novel. They were going to show the trailer. The movie was shot conventionally and then animated on top of that by hand. The director and the writer were there and said they had a big surprise. Everyone thought it was going to be Keanu Reeves, but it turned out to be this animatronic Philip K. Dick. It was programmed with pre-recorded responses. About halfway through the panel it went berserk. I think half of its head blew off, and then it just kind of slouched over.

Who would be your dream guest in the future?

Sean Astin. I loved him in *Goonies*, the *Lord of the Rings* movies, and season two of *Stranger Things*. I've talked to his agent a couple of times, but he charges the same fee whether he does one, two or three days. He would be great because he has strong ties to this region. His mom Patty Duke was from this area, so there are a lot of people around here who have interacted with him. He would be a great draw.

OK, now it's all you: What is the one knock-'em-dead, blow-their-socks-off fan convention story that you haven't told us yet? It can be funny, sad, scary, sexy, heart-warming, terrifying, sexy, action packed, cerebral, sexy or gross. Did I mention it could be sexy?

One year, I think it was 2012, our fourth or fifth show, and everything was going great. All the attendees were in, the box office had enough change, which is often a problem, and everyone was happy. Then, a fire alarm went off. We had no choice but to take it seriously. The volunteers and I got everyone out, but then a volunteer ran up and said one guy refused to leave. It was a vendor who had a glass case full of rare, first appearance golden age comics. He asked if I could guarantee the value of his books if he left them, and I said of course not. He said he wasn't going. I told him to take his damn comics with him, and he suddenly realized he could just take them out of the case and slip them under his coat. The fire department came and checked everything out, and eventually found out that it was an emergency door that was faulty. The alarm would go off even if you just leaned on it instead of when it was opened. The community college we were renting space from knew about it and didn't bother telling us. We had to wait a long time to get back in. Lots of people just left. We had to move the cosplay contest up one hour and ended up closing two hours early.

Have you had any international attendees?

We get Canadians all the time. Last week I got an email from Ireland. The guy was going to be in the region anyway and wanted to confirm that Lou Ferrigno was a guest. He had been booked for months, so I said yes. The guy was so excited because he figures it will be the only opportunity in his life to meet him.

What keeps you going, organizing your shows per year, year after year?

Every year I want to do better. After the first year, I wrote in a journal 16 things I wanted to do better the next year. The second year, there were only three items on the list. Last year, we went from a one-day show to a two-day show, and I was complaining to my wife that we should have done a better job communicating with security when the a.m. shift changed to the p.m. shift, and she just said, "Why not do that tomorrow?" I had already forgotten I could make changes the next day instead of next year. I always want to top myself. People expect it.

Dave O'Hare

Dave O'Hare is the front man for Garden State Comic Fest in New Jersey, a convention he helped found. This great family-oriented show emphasizes comic and comic creators but also brings in great celebrities, including top voice actors. The organizers emphasize the need to keep the cost reasonable and affordable so that families can keep going to it. They are proud to call it the best Comic Con in New Jersey. The show is produced in both Atlantic City and Morristown.

Can you give us a quick list of the fan conventions you have organized or attended?

I am the co-owner along with Sal Zurzolo of Garden State Comic Fest, GSCF: Great Adventure Edition, and Cosplay Collectible Con (C3).

What is the strangest thing you have seen asked to be autographed?

A body part for a tattoo and I also saw a guy bring a piece of sheet rock in from his house.

What is the most inappropriate thing a fan has done or said at one of your conventions? What about by a celebrity guest?

Honestly, we have some of the best fans out there with really no problems. We did have a fan try to steal something. He was caught, and we made sure to get the walk of shame with the police through the convention as a warning to all others. We have had nothing but positive experiences with our higher profile guests.

What about the flipside? What is the sweetest or most touching thing a fan has said or done at one of your shows?

I have been stopped by fans out on the street to say thank you for GSCF which is very humbling to me as it is because of the fans that our conventions are so good.

You interact with fans and vendors at conventions. What is the strangest thing someone has tried to sell at one of your shows?

Once saw a vendor selling a Hi-C Ecto Cooler juice box for $10 each as a joke and they both sold.

Your show features celebrities from different media and genres. How do fans of different sub-genres interact with each other? Have you seen any funny or shocking confrontations between fans over the years?

Not at our shows as everyone gets along great. But I did see a man and a woman once get into a slap fight at NYCC as they were arguing over who dressed as Link from *Legend of Zelda* better. The woman kicked his butt, haha!

When I was at the Calgary comic book convention, a 400-pound guy stepped on my foot and I yelled out "Jesus Christ!" A cosplayer dressed as Jesus Christ (at least I think it was a cosplayer) promptly appeared and offered to heal me. What is your personal WTF story from any convention?

I know the cosplayer Jesus. He is a cosplayer, right? Haha! I have seen it all! The one that stands out the most was my girlfriend was asked to take a selfie with a fan and instead of hitting the camera button they hit the gallery button, and let's just say there were quite a few inappropriate pictures of the fan in question at home which left us both laughing and a little weirded out...

What experiences have you had with fans who know far more about the celebrities of your various conventions than the celebrities themselves? How do various stars deal with that?

So far, every guest we have had at one of our shows has been the utmost professional with fans, but sometimes you do have to move some along.

What is your average convention attendee like, and which person really surprised you by being a fan?

They are the best!! We have had fans that are lawyers, doctors, police, you name it. I was surprised to see a real-life nun at one of our shows.

What about haters? Have people come to your conventions just to say how much they hate pop culture or your particular guests?

No matter what you do you always get the one person that nothing is good enough for. I am not complaining, it just happens. We try to make sure everyone has a great time as we feel it is more than just a show.

What other celebrity encounters have you had at conventions? Feel free to tell us any funny, sexy and/or terrifying close encounters you have had.

I had a celeb once ask me for a picture. That was cool!

Have you ever been mistaken for someone else at a convention, and thought "why the Hell did you think I was them?" Have you had any celebrity guests mistaken for other people?

Cannot say that I have, but we do have a volunteer that looked like me (a little skinnier) and people were mistaking him for me which was cool as I was able to be in two places at one time :)

What is the one that got away? Which celebrity were you this close to getting only to have them pull out at the last nanosecond?

We had one this year that we REALLY wanted to be part of GSCF but due to personal issues, which was very sad, they were not able to make it. I cannot give a name as we are trying again.

Cosplay has become an art form. What costume at any convention has totally blown you away and amazed you with its high quality and detail? What is the all-time worst costume you have seen?

I have seen some amazing costumes such as the Hulkbuster done by Extreme Costumes which really stands out and so many others. It truly is an art form unto itself. As for the worst, I will admit I have seen some real failures but it's the ones who don't try, like a bag on their head. I wonder why they even bother.

What super fans have you encountered whose whole lives have been consumed with one topic or movie they live for?

We have quite a few die-hards that I have met. I love their passion.

Comic book conventions have gone from small gatherings to huge multimedia showcases. How has your show in particular changed and how has the type of celebrity who appears at them changed?

Garden State is really a comic book convention, in every aspect an anti-con con if you will. We base it on comic collectibles and the creators them are our true stars. We do bring in between one and three celebrity or movie guests each year but never to take away, but to only add to the atmosphere.

Before you became a convention organizer you were a fan. Ever have any true fanboy moments encountering celebrities before you became one of their employers?

My biggest was meeting Larry Hama who wrote *GI Joe*, as that was my childhood. I still get giddy around him.

Do you get many international fans at your shows, or fans of foreign pop culture?

Yes, we do. As we are a top collector show, we get fans and collectors from all over the world at GSCF and we are proud of that.

What would your dream guest be in the future?

There are so many, but I would say Geoff Johns, Alex Ross, and Peter Dinklage.

Have you ever had a celebrity make strange demands on you in order to be a guest at one of your shows?

Define "strange" haha! They all have little things, but nothing too far gone.

OK, now it's all you: What is the one knock-'em-dead, blow-their-socks-off fan convention story that you haven't told us yet? It can be funny, sad, scary, sexy, heart-warming, terrifying, sexy, action packed, cerebral, sexy or gross. Did I mention it could be sexy?

Sorry, those stories are not for print LOL!

What keeps you going, organizing multiple shows per year, year after year?

The love of it and of course the fans!

I have been to conventions where there is one vendor who seems badly out of place, like they didn't know what kind of show they were buying a table at. Have you had any experiences like that?

We have not but I did hear a sex toy shop set up at Wizard Philly one year. That does seem to be out of place, especially since most shows are very family friendly.

DAVE O'HARE'S LEAST FAVORITE COSPLAY ATTEMPTS:

UNKNOWN COMIC

ED THE SOCK

JASON FROM FRIDAY THE 13TH PART 2

KILLER FROM THE TOWN THAT DREADED SUNDOWN

THE WORST THING ABOUT BEING CAUGHT STEALING AT GARDEN STATE COMIC FESTIVAL IS BEING FORCED TO POSE FOR ALL THE PHOTO OPS.

Ben Penrod

Awesome Con is Washington, D.C.'s awesome comic book convention. Among other things it is cosplay nirvana and holder of the record for most cosplayers gathering as comic book characters. It emphasizes strong comic book talent but also brings in top-name celebrities. Founder Ben Penrod's responses are shorter than many in this book, but he also took time during one of his busy conventions, so hats off to him.

Can you give us a quick list of the fan conventions you have organized or attended?

I have organized the Annapolis Comic-Con, Southern Maryland Comic-Con, and Awesome Con. I've attended nearly every major fan convention in North America and hundreds of smaller conventions.

What is the strangest thing you have seen asked to be autographed?

It's always strange when people ask to have their body autographed and then get the autograph tattooed on them.

What is the most inappropriate thing a fan has done or said at one of your conventions? What about by a celebrity guest?

I don't think we've had any issues with guests; as far as fans, I really can't think of much. I think someone got drunk once before they came to the con and fell on the escalator and had to be removed by security.

What about the flipside? What is the sweetest or most touching thing a fan has said or done at one of your shows?

I've met fans who are engaged or married who met at Awesome Con. That's the coolest thing, in my opinion!!

You interact with fans and vendors at conventions. What is the strangest thing someone has tried to sell at one of your shows?

Everything that is sold at Awesome Con is probably pretty normal to whoever is a fan of it, but is strange to someone else. We are also pretty strict about making sure that our vendors are only selling things that are relevant to Awesome Con's attendees.

Your show features celebrities from different media and genres. How do fans of different sub-genres interact with each other? Have you seen any funny or shocking confrontations between fans over the years?

No, people in fandom are overwhelmingly tolerant. They understand what it means to be passionate about something, and generally they respect that in others, too. I've seen some funny cosplay interactions between heroes and villains, but that's always in good fun.

Comic book conventions have gone from small gatherings to huge multimedia showcases. How has your show in particular changed and how has the type of celebrity who appears at them changed?

Awesome Con hasn't changed in tone or in spirit, but it is a much larger event with a lot more different things going on. We always add elements to the show every year, but not in any way that would change the foundation of what Awesome Con is.

Before you became a convention organizer you were a fan. Ever have any true fanboy moments encountering celebrities before you became one of their employers?

For me, I'm pretty lucky that I don't really get "star-struck." It's fun to be around the people who create the things I love, but I know they're mostly just regular people. I did get to talk to Billy West about the *Futurama* episode, "Jurassic Bark," which was pretty cool.

Photo ops are a convention favorite. Tell us about the more memorable ones you have seen.

I've seen people pop the question to their significant other in a photo op, with a confused celebrity looking on!

Do you get many international fans at your shows, or fans of foreign pop culture?

Absolutely! With our history of bringing in international celebrity guests, we also see international fans traveling to meet them.

Who would be your dream guest in the future?

Bill Murray.

THE DANGER OF PROPOSING DURING A PHOTO OP.

Kevin Scarpino

Keven Scarpino is not just a local television personality from Cleveland. He is the world's most famous local television personality from Cleveland.

Keven Scarpino is Son of Ghoul, and Son of Ghoul is the longest running horror host still on television, going on 33 years.

At one point in time, live horror hosts were a fixture of local television. There were dozens of them with a variety of ghoulish sounding names, but as local TV programming died off, so did they (which is ironic, because most of them were supposed to be undead).

Elvira started as one, but then went on to become whatever she is today (Actress? World's oldest pinup model? Annoying?). Joe Flaherty, as Count Floyd, parodied one on SCTV. Lisa Marie, as Vampira, portrayed one of the first ones in the movie *Ed Wood*. *Mystery Science Theatre* and *Movies from Space* are probably the closest you've seen, but that is like saying seeing a bird is the same as seeing a dinosaur because they are distantly related to the original, but much smaller, less cool, and they crap everywhere.

But Son of Ghoul is the real deal, still appearing every week to mock the bad movies he shows and entertain (?) his fans with comedy (??) in between segments.

Check out his website and the clips of him on You Tube. Better yet, check him out at one of his many personal appearances and try to convince your local TV station that they need a live horror host, because who wants to run second best to Cleveland?

Can you give us a quick list of the fan conventions you have appeared at, as both a fan and celebrity guest?

As a fan... Beatlefest in New York City, New Jersey, Cleveland and Akron. I've appeared at The Monster Bash (PA), Frightvision, Cinema Wasteland, Ghoulardifest, Monsterfestmania, Akron Comic Con, Haunted Hotel (all Ohio), Horrorhound (Indiana), Thrillville (California), and a few more that I forgot the convention's names, but they were in Chicago, Baltimore (MD) and one more somewhere in Kentucky.

What is the strangest thing you have been asked to autograph?

A bare female breast. (Although not too strange).

What is the most inappropriate thing a fan has done or said to you?

I was appearing as an MC at an all-night Pro Football Hall Of Fame concert featuring all local bands. During one of my slots on stage some irate fan in the crowd started swearing and clenching his fist at me, trying to jump up on stage to attack me. I had to notify the security to have him removed. To this day I have no idea what his problem was. Maybe he wasn't a fan at all.

What about the flipside? What is the sweetest or most touching thing a fan has said or done for you?

Countless things like being taken out to breakfast, lunch and dinners, being sent money orders and cash and gifts for no reason. Last year I was appearing at a convention and two senior grandparents approached me with their mentally challenged grandson. The grandfather told me that his grandson was pretty much a hopeless case, very hard to communicate with and understand. But for some reason, he fell in love with my show, and it has lifted his spirits and somehow awakened his awareness a lot. The grandfather thanked me for making a difference in his grandson's life. Left me kind of speechless.

Have you had people come up to you dressed as Son of Ghoul?

Many times, adults and children.

When I was at the Calgary comic book convention, a 400 pound guy stepped on my foot and I yelled out "Jesus Christ!" A cosplayer dressed as Jesus Christ

(at least I think it was a cosplayer) promptly appeared and offered to heal me. What is your personal WTF story from any convention?

Once I had a self-proclaimed witch approach me at a convention and insisted that great fortune is coming my way. To this date, nothing.

You have been a horror host for more than 30 years. What experiences have you had with fans who know far more about your career than you could ever hope to know? How do you deal with that situation?

Hey now, it's 34 continuous years on the air on June 13th 2020. People always ask me or tell me about something I said or did or maybe a sound effect I used in one of the movies. I'm always honest, whether I remember it or not. I have had parents come up and tell me that their child video tapes each show and gets very concerned about why a prop on the set has been moved to another location on the set from week to week. I normally tell them that they need to take their child to a doctor.

What other celebrity encounters have you had at conventions? Feel free to tell us any funny, sexy and/or terrifying close encounters you have had.

I usually don't bother the celebrity guests at most conventions but I have had the great fortune to meet or interview most of them. I have had more than great times with some such as Arch Hall Jr. and the late Ben Chapman. Once at The Monster Bash I was set up right next to the late, great Richard Kiel. All weekend he sat and sold many autographed photos of himself and did quite well. At one point I had to ask him..."Richard, why don't you have a set of those Jaws teeth handy in your pocket because I'm more than sure that everybody at this convention, vendor or patron would gladly pay greatly to have their photo snapped with the famous "Jaws"? You could make a bigger boat load of money." He looked at me and said, "You see, that would just be a hassle." I still don't understand that comment but I will tell you one thing, if I had the role of "Jaws" from two James Bond films in my back pocket, I would of had a fresh roll of tin foil under my table and would've gladly foiled my teeth up in a jiffy to pull in those BIG BUCKS.

Have you ever been mistaken for someone else at a convention, and thought "why the Hell did you think I was them?"

I was once confused to be Svengoolie and I thought "why the hell do you think I'm him? I wear glasses and my eyes don't look like a raccoon's". Plus, most importantly, I'm funny.

Cosplay has become an art form. What costume at any convention has totally blown you away and amazed you with its high quality and detail? What is the all-time worst costume you have seen?

I have seen quite a lot of amazing costumes over the years. I suppose it would be a home-made costume. I remember some woman won a costume contest one year dressed as the woman's head from the classic film *The Brain That Wouldn't Die*, all wrapped up, blood pan and all. The worst has to be some dude came dressed as a used condom (no pun intended).

You have been photographed thousands of times. What is your favorite photo with a fan, and what was the one request that made you shake your head, laugh or throw up a little in your mouth?

I was appearing at a parade and in the line up area some parent insisted that I hold his child in my arms for a photo. The problem was that the kid was terrified of me and was balling his little eyes out during the photo but it's a great shot nevertheless. Another of my favorites appeared in a news-paper. I was in another parade sitting on the back of a fire engine water truck. The firemen supplied me with a small but powerful water hose that I could spray at the people on the parade route. The next year I did the parade again and some kid came prepared with his water blaster and when my truck went by him, I just happened to be looking to the other side of the street and totally missed him. A newspaper photographer snapped a photo of the little kid crying because he didn't get to squirt me. It's one of my favorite shots.

Gender bender cosplay continues to get more and more popular. Have you met a female version of yourself? What was that like?

I met a female at an appearance dressed as me. Not good, to say the least.

Before you became a celebrity you were a fan. Ever have any true fanboy moments encountering celebrities before you became one?

The very first celebrity I got to almost meet was the famous Ghoulardi, Ernie Anderson. In 1965 he appeared at my local Stark county fair. It was a Thursday evening in September. I was 10 years old and with my par-ents. Ghoulardi was scheduled to appear around 7 P.M. The grandstands and the entire area were packed with people watching the horse races (that was in progress) and waiting for Ghoulardi. The horse race was running longer than scheduled and Ghoulardi must have become impatient to make his appearance. I remember that the horses came around for their last lap of the race and at that point Ghoulardi appeared from under the grandstands and proceeded to walk across the racetrack headed to a small podium where he was to appear. He was mobbed by a large swarm of fans who jumped over the fences onto the racetrack. Excited fans pulled his fright wig and his phony beard off of his face as he crossed the track. Police quickly scrambled to help him to safety and to clear all the people from the racetrack because the horse race was not over and the horses were in full gallop and coming hard around the bend headed to the finish line right where everybody was standing. The people were cleared out in the nick of time and the race was now over. They let everybody back onto the race track to rush the podium. Ghoulardi did the appearance without his now stolen fright wig and beard. I made a poster that said "Ghoulardi for future babysitter" and lightly mounted my original Ghoulardi autographed card to it. He spotted me holding up my poster and said, "Hey kid, gimme that poster." I handed it up to him and he held it up and read it over the mic, then tossed it to the floor. I then realized that my authentic Ghoulardi autograph was now laying on the floor and lost forever. When his appearance was over, he headed to a black limo and climbed in the back seat and sat in the center. There were older men in suits sitting on both sides of him. I saw two older kids run up to the limo and they said, "Hey Ghoulardi, how about a handshake?" He obliged. The kids parted and I was standing there, I held my hand out to get my handshake and at that point the window in the limo started to go up. I quickly pulled my hand away and Ghoulardi just looked at me and shrugged his shoulders, I got no handshake and the limo pulled away. Bummer!

You have been interviewed and done panels at conventions. What are the funniest, strangest and most thought provoking questions you have encountered?
People always ask me how I got started or what's my favorite horror movie that I have shown which always takes some thought. Nothing that really stands out. As usual my head is empty.

You are constantly on the road. What is the hardest part of that and your funniest story about it?

I guess lodging costs. One year at a Convention, to save money, I brought along an air mattress and roughed it and slept in my van for three nights. The hotel had a shower and bathroom that I had access to so that problem was solved. The funny thing was at The Monster Bash convention I was selected to win the Forrest J Ackerman award. I knew nothing about being selected and the award was handed out around 11 P.M. or midnight. Being up all day, I was all pooped out and when they were announcing my name to receive my award, I was nowhere to be found. I was sawing logs in my van. Just my luck, I missed my honor moment again. They did give me my trophy the next day because they are very honourable.

Now it's all you: What is the one knock-'em-dead, blow-their-socks-off fan convention story that you haven't told us yet? It can be funny, sad, scary, sexy, heart-warming, terrifying, sexy, action packed, cerebral, sexy or gross. Did I mention it could be sexy? I'm trying to sell some books here.

This is not a convention story but back in 1986 I was hired to judge a Halloween costume contest at a local shopping mall. They had a video arcade in the mall which sponsored my show and we did a commercial on TV about entering the contest. The prize was a year's worth of free video games at the arcade and some cash. There were adult and children's prizes awarded. The contest drew a gigantic crowd and I showed up with my then girlfriend who stood in the back of the room during the contest with her usual scowl. Mind you there were loads of parents, kids and adults in this contest. One at a time each contestant walked up front to the stage to show me their costume. At one point some very attractive adult woman approached the stage wearing a floor length Uncle Fester type black coat. She was facing me and the audience could only see the back of her coat. She looked up at me and said, "Do I win?" and opened her coat just a bit to show me that she was completely naked. Nobody else in the room saw this eye opener but me. I looked up at my girlfriend standing and still scowling in the back of the room who had no idea what I was seeing. I smiled at her then I looked down at the exposed woman and said, "Very nice. Very nice indeed!" and it was. What could I say or do? She didn't win and I have never run into her again. Dammit.

7. SON OF GHOUL HAS NEVER POSED NUDE, MAKING THE WORLD A PRETTIER PLACE.

4: SON OF GHOUL HAS NEVER DATED ELVIS, ALTHOUGH HE CAME PRETTY CLOSE A FEW TIMES.

3: FOR $45, ELVIRA WILL SEND YOU AN AUTOGRAPHED PICTURE. FOR $45, SON OF GHOUL WILL COME TO YOUR HOUSE AND STAY AS LONG AS YOU WANT.

Spock Vegas

Paul Forest became Spock Vegas, the world's greatest (and tallest|) Mr. Spock cosplayer in 2012. Originally appearing in Las Vegas' Freemont Street, he went on to become a hit at fan conventions around the world.

Can you give us a quick list of the fan conventions you have appeared at, as both a fan and celebrity guest?
Well let's see, I have attended 81 exactly in three years of exclusively going to cons, completed just now. So, I started September 12th, 2014 with the Montreal Comic Con, then a month later "Destination Star Trek" 2014 at the Excel in London, England and New York Comic Con. I went to small cons like Evansville CC and did pretty much all the big ones in the US like San Diego, Comikaze, and some in the UK like London Film & Comic Con, and so many more cons of all types in the US. Plus, almost all of Canada's cons in each province. The farthest one was Dubai Comic Con.

What is the strangest thing you have been asked to autograph?
Unfortunately, nothing strange, although this may happen to big stars. Just a miniature replica of the Enterprise, with very small signatures from all remaining *TOS* cast members. Also, a replica of a *Star Trek* pod owned by Martin Netter of Filmwelt, also signed by the original crew. I would not say strange, but very special items.

What is the most inappropriate thing a fan has done or said to you?
Out of the hundreds of negative comments stupid people could come up with, the worst occasion was when a girl one day pulled and removed one of my ears. It was rude, invasive, an assault basically. But she was drunk, so who can judge her actions? The funniest comment was published after a girl took a photo with me: she wrote, "It's Spak from Star Wars".

What about the flipside? What is the sweetest or most touching thing a fan has said or done for you?
That feels a lot better to answer. Out of the hundreds of thousands of positive comments or actions, receiving two gifts at each of the 81 comic cons in three years so far, like clockwork, is the most fascinating thing to mention. Sometimes I am given an article related to Nimoy, but most of the time a handmade portrait or piece of art is the most heartfelt gift one can offer. So many gifts, so many comments, so many good memories.

You're a big man (around 6 feet 8 inches), and you play a character who was a total badass and master of the Vulcan nerve pinch. Has anyone ever challenged you to fight when you are in the Spock character?

No one ever dared. I'm 6'8", so they go the pacifist way with me. Some just try the pinch on me, but I say, "It doesn't work on Vulcans", so they laugh and keep walking.

You are an action figure! How does it feel to have your own action figure and see yourself shrunk down to miniature size?

I represent an icon, so I was offered twice to pose for fun for promotional uses of my portrayal of Spock. I don't think they sold any more than a few to my close friends. All I know is I got one for free from both companies.

What experiences have you had with fans who know far more about your character than you could ever hope to know? How do you deal with that situation?

I have said often that real Trekkies know a lot more than me. They speak Klingon and Vulcan, they know everything about every show, and a lot more about every culture. But I let them talk. They are teaching others when they meet another knowledgeable fan they can discuss with. And who better than Spock as your audience? Maybe they expect me to know as much as them, or even more. I just use what I know and agree with the rest. Anyway, they seem happy when they leave.

You have been able to meet members of the original Star Trek cast as well as the more recent movies as a result of being Spock Vegas. What was it like meeting Shatner, Quinto, and all the rest, including Nimoy himself?

It's unreal to see someone on TV all those years and then to meet them. Everyone knows that. That's why comic cons are so popular, they are right there. I wanted to meet them, yes, but to show them Spock as he was always has been my ultimate thrill. To see their reactions. But what they felt inside I don't know. Takei was staring at me with his mouth open. Nimoy laughed, both times. Shatner shouted and gave me the knuckle. Nichols was startled but kept smiling.

Have you been to Vulcan (as in Vulcan, Alberta) yet? Nimoy did a famous "homecoming" there a few years ago.

I have never been but was casually invited over the years while on Fremont Street by at least 40 people that lived in Vulcan, Alberta, so almost the whole town. I have no intention of going anytime soon.

What other celebrity encounters have you had at conventions? Feel free to tell us any funny, sexy and/or terrifying close encounters you have had.
I have met a hundred for sure so far, from other *Star Trek* shows, movies and TV shows. It's a book in itself. The most popular photo was with Gene Simmons with 12k likes on his Facebook page.

Cosplay has become an art form. What costume at any convention has totally blown you away and amazed you with its high quality and detail? What is the all-time worst costume you have seen?
There are too many good ones, and I wouldn't know their names. But I agree that quality is important if one wants to call himself a cosplayer. Passion determines whether one's cosplay is worthy of the name. It can be duct tape and cardboard when money is an issue, but it's the intention that counts, and even those sometimes can be quite impressive. The worst I've seen is a $25 Halloween costume of a Ninja Turtle.

You have been photographed thousands of times. What is your favourite photo with a fan, and what was the one request that made you shake your head, laugh or throw up a little in your mouth?
I figure more than 100k times. I always refused stupid photos, even for $100. I'm not there to joke around with drunk or rude people. I represent a man and a respected character. If the idea of a photo does not fit either, I usually propose the normal Vulcan salute instead. In 7 years, for sure there were a few weird ones, and especially when the demand came from a female, I guess I was more receptive. But there is nothing out there that would make me or him look bad.

Gender bender cosplay continues to get more and more popular. Have you met a female version of your character at conventions? What was that like?
I always say "I love the haircut." I met maybe 20 Spock females characters and they are in love with Spock and they absolutely want a photo with Spock. It's a compliment to the character that anyone could want to be him

for a while. Women or even kids, as their parents dress them up as Spock for the weekend.

Before you became a celebrity you were a fan. Ever have any true fanboy moments encountering celebrities before you became one?

Well, I'm a somewhat recognizable cosplayer; I am no celebrity. I always called myself "the poor VIP" throughout my life. I met and shook hands with Robert DeNiro at a private party my friend organized during film-ing of *The Heist* in Montreal. I shook Peter Gabriel's hand at a show, just because I was tall. I met many local artists in my "fanboy times" where I grew up in Montreal when I was younger. I drove a limousine and met a lot of very interesting people back then. In recent memory, the whole crew of *Enterprise*, and other *Star Trek* shows, Gowan, Gene Simmons, Norman Reedus, Christopher Lloyd (Doc), Deb from *Dexter*, Lou Ferrigno (Hulk), Peter Mayhew (Chewie), David Prowse (Vader), Neve Campbell, Julian Sands . . . the list is way too long. I walked the celebrity room dressed as Spock at almost every show I've been to, so you can imagine all the hands I shook.

You have been interviewed and done panels at conventions. What are the funniest, strangest and most thought-provoking questions you have encountered?

Although questions are often about my extreme height or my likeness to Spock, my favourite questions are when people ask about why people dress up at cons. My answer always includes the fact that cons are a place of no judgement, where one can be himself in any way he chooses to, dressed up or not. I also often get questions about my career and my extensive travels to give Spock back to the public, for them to enjoy seeing Spock, who is often their favourite character, at 81 Comic Cons so far.

You have literally gone around the world to do fan conventions. What's it like doing fan conventions in Europe, the Middle East, and elsewhere?

Yes, Dubai Comic Con was an amazing experience. To be invited as a guest is the best feeling a cosplayer can ask for. Being recognized as the best Spock on the other side of the planet is a great compliment. The public was very receptive, intelligent, curious and full of energy. That is the third goal of my mission, to travel without paying for it. The first goal

I mentioned above, to give *Star Trek* fans a chance to feel the experience of seeing Spock one last time, and the second being donating as much I can to charity.

You are constantly on the road. What is the hardest part about travel, and your funniest story from being on the road?

Traveling economy often means 16-hour days in transit, before and after the con. So the whole day is spent getting to your room on Thursday night, to be ready at 10am for the Friday morning door opening time. It's not easy, but once you get there, it's always fun.

Ever get asked if you are going through Pon Farr?

At least once every show, somebody jokes about that mysterious period that comes every seven years, especially when I am in the presence of a beauty and the guy next to her sees me smile or start flirting with her. There's always something about females that will make me go out of character, or let's say, reveal my human side, that the Vulcan in me can't control. This happens way more often than every 7 years in my case. How about many times per day! But I kind of stay in control, and I don't smash monitors or highjack planes to go back to my planet to mate. Actually, I think I might be a real Vulcan.

Star Trek had its 50th anniversary. How did you take part in the celebrations?

I became Spock Vegas on February 28th, 2011, so just in time to be known enough in the biz and prepared for the big moment of *Star Trek TOS* in 2016. It was Spock Vegas's best year and I don't think I'll ever top that. I guested everywhere and cons were actually reaching out to me, instead of the usual, "Hey, look here, guest me!! Everyone loves Spock, it'll be good for your show, the media loves me, they chose me as the poster boy for this and that show, etc., etc.", only to receive a negative answer like, "You have zero credits, we only invite artists", or even no reply at all, to three email reminders. For once and finally, I was seen by the con owners as a valuable asset for their show. I was even featured as a "fan dressing up as Spock" in the Adam Nimoy film about his father, *For the Love of Spock*, where I talk about what impact Nimoy had through his character. I'm just sad Nimoy died the year before and didn't get to live that amazing year.

OK, now it's all you: What is the one knock-'em-dead, blow-their-socks-off fan convention story that you haven't told us yet? It can be funny, sad, scary, sexy, heart-warming, terrifying, sexy, action packed, cerebral, sexy or gross. Did I mention it could be sexy?

I'll keep those ones for my own book. You know, there can't be only one, cause my memory is a mess of a million episodes of fun and experiences, a big blur lasting three years - well, I would say seven including my four Vegas years on Fremont Street. I'll say this, though: the smiles. I'm rich with the most incredible smiles I get from fans. The laughter when they see me. The range of emotions going through their faces tells me so much about how they feel, and often joined by hugs, jumping or shaking like leaves. And to think I've only personally witnessed maybe 10% of those reactions. It is a great privilege to look like a man that was loved by all, and to be seen as the best, and to receive all those comments and gifts. To have grown men really shake your hand, with a tear in their eyes, saying, "You nailed it", or "You made my weekend", or "You're the best thing I've seen at this show", that's my most heart-warming dream come true. That's pretty knock-em-dead sexy.

J. Tanooki a.k.a. Jamie from Winnipeg

J. Tanooki is a Canadian cosplayer and model who has been cosplaying for over 13 years. She actively joined the cosplay community in 2014, attending events throughout the year in her hometown of Winnipeg, as well as other cities in Canada and the U.S. She has also been able to bring her passion to her local community through assisting in fundraising events for cancer awareness, modelling for photography students at a local college, and contributing to a nerd culture website offering her insight into the cosplay and convention community.

That is her official biography, but what I can add is that J. Tanooki, a.k.a. Jamie from WInnipeg, was an extremely hard person to interview at a convention, and not because she was not willing to talk. She is an extremely open and approachable person who holds nothing back. It was difficult because she was so popular that she was constantly in demand by her fans to sell them prints, pose for selfies, or more often, just talk about cosplaying, her social media posts or anything in general. She is a great cosplayer and a great lady. One of her prints is on the following page, and although it captures her beauty, it does not do justice to her great personality and approachability; to discover that, you should actively seek her out at one of her personal appearances.

Can you give us a quick list of the fan conventions you have appeared at, as both a fan and celebrity guest?
I have cosplayed at 15 different conventions in North America, and most of those multiple times. My all-time favorite was the Edmonton Expo. I was part of a group cosplay with a bunch of friends

What is the strangest thing you have been asked to autograph?

I was doing a charity event where my photo fee went to the charity. Someone grabbed the poster advertising the event and had me autograph that as well.

What is the most inappropriate thing a fan has done or said to you?

It seemed really bad at the time, but turned out to be a misunderstanding. I was doing a body paint show, and besides my costume I had on body paint so I was colored like an old comic book, with a background color and then dots all over me. A guy came up to me, looked down my cleavage, and said, "Are those real?" I started to lose it on him, and he was so embarrassed because he was actually talking about my body paint! He thought all the dots on me were tattoos! I also do boudoir modelling, so it usually takes a lot to shock me.

What about the flipside? What is the sweetest or most touching thing a fan has said or done for you?

I had streamed on Twitch the complete process of me making one of my own costumes. A man came to a show and said he had been so inspired that he had gone out, bought a sewing machine, learned how to use it, and was now getting caught up in the whole cosplay culture. It was great because he was having a great time as a result of watching my demonstration.

When I was at the Calgary comic book convention, a 400 pound guy stepped on my foot and I yelled out "Jesus Christ!" A cosplayer dressed as Jesus Christ (at least I think it was a cosplayer) promptly appeared and offered to heal me. What is your personal WTF story from any convention?

My WTF story is the most inspirational thing that has ever happened to me. I had just gone through a job loss. I had to leave my job due to medical problems, which were mental health related. I have always been very open and honest about that. It was especially devastating because I had been saving up for something on my bucket list, namely a trip to the Anime Ex in Los Angeles. My doctor thought it would be good for me to go because it would be a good "reset button" for my life, a new starting point, but I just couldn't afford it. I thought talking about how I felt would help me feel better, so I started posting about it on Facebook and Instagram. It was a real icebreaker. Lots of people started sharing their similar stories. I never asked anyone for money, but someone who was following me found my donation account, and I started getting all of these notifications that people were sending money. All of these strangers banded together, supported me, and got me on my dream trip.

Have you ever been mistaken for someone else at a convention, and thought "why the Hell did you think I was them?"

Usually, people mistake the character I'm cosplaying for someone else. I was mistaken repeatedly for Jessica Nigiri at one show. We look nothing alike, but we were both at RTX the same year cosplaying the same character, Arcade Miss Fortune, so as soon as people saw the character, they assumed I was her, the most famous cosplayer on the planet.

Last Son Cosplay a.k.a. Jeff Thorpe of Toronto

Jeff, a.k.a The Last Son, is a cosplay model and entertainer who produces epic photoshoots. He is known for both his Disney prince/villain recreations as well as various superhero cosplays. Closing in on 40,000 followers on Instagram he has made quite the name for himself in the Disney cosplay community. The Last Son has been cosplaying for 4 years, performing at conventions as well as volunteering for charitable organizations such as SickKids. He is also known to serenade his fans with classic Disney tunes, and generally stays in character while in costume, giving con-goers the full immersive experience.

He is renowned for starring in and producing comprehensive photoshoots involving dozens of talented cosplayers and the talented photographer Alex Rose; these photoshoots have achieved internet acclaim and viral status, being viewed by hundreds of thousands of people worldwide. While he does not produce his own costumes, he works with and supports various talented crafts people in the community such as the internationally renowned Violet Love and Jason Evans.

That is Jeff Thorpe's official bio from one of his many costumed appearances. He has built a good reputation for himself in a field dominated by women. At six feet five inches tall, he is both an imposing figure but one that children are instantly drawn to; if anyone was born to play larger than life characters, it was him.

Can you give us a quick list of the fan conventions you have appeared at, as both a fan and celebrity guest?

I've been to lots as a cosplayer, including the Celebrity Sailor Moon show, Woodbridge Heroes and many in the Toronto area. I work closely with the Toronto Children's Hospital in organizing character appearances there. I also appear at private events like birthday parties.

What is the strangest thing you have been asked to autograph?

I don't get asked for a lot of autographs. As a male cosplayer, I have to sell myself more in terms of promotion. It takes a lot of elbow grease.

What is the most inappropriate thing a fan has done or said to you?

At conventions, I have no problems. I act as a cosplay vigilante in protecting the girl cosplayers, who can get a lot of harassment. Outside of conventions, it only happened once at a gay pride parade I appeared at as Superman. Gay men are very nice, but they can get a little too friendly with their hands.

What about the flipside? What is the sweetest or most touching thing a fan has said or done for you?

The most touching experience I've had was at the sick kids' hospital with a little girl who was terminal with cancer and had a week or two to live. I dressed up as Prince Phillip from Sleeping Beauty and I got every Disney princess cosplayer I could find. There were about 9 of them. We all went to see her as a group, and her jaw kept dropping lower and lower as we came in. She finally asked her mom if she had died and gone to Heaven. Everyone in the room was crying after that. She died within two weeks of that. I love working with the hospital, but it can get really heavy. You have to stay in character the whole time, like the character actors at Disneyland, but you're dealing with kids in wheelchairs who are going through a lot. The kids love it and grin from ear to ear.

When I was at the Calgary comic book convention, a 400 pound guy stepped on my foot and I yelled out "Jesus Christ!" A cosplayer dressed as Jesus Christ (at least I think it was a cosplayer) promptly appeared and offered to heal me. What is your personal WTF story from any convention?

It was actually coming home from a convention in the greater Toronto area. I had gotten caught in a bad traffic jam on the 401 highway and it was after 2 a.m. I was driving home and passing through a bad area of town when I saw a woman walking who was obviously terrified and looking over her shoulder constantly. I stopped and rolled down the window and asked if she needed me to call 911. She said there was no time to do that because someone was following close behind her and had been for blocks. I looked, and there was this guy in a black hoodie skulking towards her, keeping to the shadow. I'm six foot five, so I figure I'll just scare him off. I jumped out of the car and yelled at him, and he took off running. It was then that I realized I was still dressed as Superman. I looked at the lady and the look on her face just said, "OK, which of these two guys is crazier?" She let me give her a ride home, but she kept her eyes on me the whole time.

Have you ever been mistaken for someone else at a convention, and thought "why the Hell did you think I was them?"
When I'm not in costume, people say I look like either Cory Feldman or Patrick Swayze. Strangely enough, people have also said that I look like Clark Kent, which is a good thing for a Superman cosplayer to hear.

When I'm in costume, people usually act like I'm the character. With kids six years old and younger, they believe that cosplayers are the characters. You are real to them. Adults can get into it too, though. I am a big karaoke enthusiast as well as a karaoke leader. I organize Disney karaoke shows and lead them as Gaston, but I only sing non-*Beauty and the Beast* songs. When I do A Whole New World from *Aladdin*, it comes off as a 70's French lounge singer. Gaston basically has the character of an obnoxious drunk frat boy, so he is perfect for karaoke. People get right into it. Women swoon and men act like his peanut gallery. I lift people on my shoulders, and everyone has a great time.

You have been photographed thousands of times. What is your favorite photo with a fan, and what was the one request that made you shake your head, laugh or throw up a little in your mouth?
Photos at conventions are usually selfies with fans and are pretty conventional. I also organize photo shoots with professional photographers that are great. We recreate scenes from movies and fans love them.

You have been interviewed and done panels at conventions. What are the funniest, strangest and most thought provoking questions you have encountered?
If I am in a panel, I usually end up hosting them. They are usually cosplay panels with lots of technical questions on how to do cosplay.

Now it's all you: What is the one knock-'em-dead, blow-their-socks-off fan convention story that you haven't told us yet? It can be funny, sad, scary, sexy, heart-warming, terrifying, sexy, action packed, cerebral, sexy or gross. Did I mention it could be sexy? I'm trying to sell some books here.

There are literally stories from every show. I was doing a show as Gaston and there were three girls there dressed as the Bindettes, who were his groupies in the movies. There is a scene in the movie where he lifts all of them at once, and I managed to lift one on each of my biceps and the third one on my shoulders. I held it for about five seconds while someone took a picture. They got off, and I saw that there was now a crowd of about 200 people around us. I said that they all had to take their pictures at once, not individually.

At a Sailor Moon show, I volunteered to help transport the celebrity guests around. I was cosplaying Tuxedo Mask, and it turned out that the parents of the actor who played Tuxedo Mask literally lived right across the street from me. He was staying with them for the show. I went there in costume, and he pointed at me and exclaimed: "See? That's who I play on TV! That's me!" Until then, they had no idea what he did for a living because they had never seen the show.

You're a big guy cosplaying tough, macho characters. Has anyone ever wanted to fight you in character?

I'm very good at using my words. I can talk my way out of anything. If someone wants to get into a conflict with me, they usually end up being friends with me.

Dyanne Thorne and Howard Maurer

Dyanne Thorne was guaranteed lifetime invitations to be a guest at fan conventions-when she appeared in a small part in the first season episode of *Star Trek: TOS*, "A Piece of the Action". However, she went on to play some of the greatest and most outrageous supervillains in the history of movies in such films as *Ilsa, She Wolf of the SS*; *Ilsa, Harem Keeper of the Oil Sheiks*; *Ilsa, Tigress of Siberia*; *Greta, the Wicked Warden*, and others. In addition to her many IMDb credits, Dyanne is an incredibly talented stage actress, having appeared in everything from regional theatre, touring productions, and Las Vegas revues.

Howard Maurer is generally credited as being one of the greatest geniuses of our time, because, let's face it, he married Dyanne Thorne when nobody else thought to do that. I mean, if Stephen Hawking was so damned smart, why didn't he ever do that?

But seriously, folks, Howie Maurer is one of the funniest people you will ever meet. He did a nightclub musical comedy act for many years, worked as a lounge singer for casinos when Frank Sinatra was playing their main room (which in Las Vegas terms is the equivalent of St. Peter's job in Heaven; you're not God, but you're as close as you can get), had hit songs in Europe and Japan, and has appeared in many movies. He has also produced films and Las Vegas revues.

These two charming people were by the far the most entertaining that I interviewed for this book. It was very fitting that they were both ordained ministers in Las Vegas. Since this interview was done, Dyanne passed away. In preparing this book, I spoke to many people who knew her and she was universally loved. The fact that she could play such despicable human beings while being so inherently sweet and good is proof of what a great actress she was. The last communication I had with her is a copy of this song that Howie wrote for her. It is a great tribute to this great lady

She's an actress, she can make your whole world shine
To watch her is like drinking vintage wine
She's an actress

She's got magic, when the things that make you cry
Seem to disappear before your very eyes
She's an actress

Looking sad is something that she never does but if she does
You can bet she'll never let it show
Feeling bad is something that she always hides deep inside
And you know she'll never let you know

Hang around her, hang around her if you could (for a while)
Hanging 'round her makes me feel so good (has to make you smile)

She's an actress, she's got magic, she's an actress

Can you give us a quick list of the fan conventions you have appeared at other than those listed on your website?
Dyanne: Our favorites are James Bialkowski's show in Canada and Ken Kish's Cinema Wasteland. We also have fan clubs all over the world, and we have been invited to Germany, Greece, Austria, Italy, Tokyo, Belgium, Norway, London, and others, but we haven't taken them up on it. We always want to go early and stay late for a few days so we can explore the country, but these small clubs can't accommodate that. I would love to go to Australia.

Howie: The first one I did was the New Jersey Chillers show. My favorite one is the Hollywood Show. I was at the last one Ernest Borgnine did and got to sit by him. He was 90 and absolutely charming. Unfortunately, that was just before he died. Bruce Dern was at that show too. I was at a great Hollywood Show in Tampa once. They had 16 great stars booked, but some guys were so disappointed that they weren't getting enough fans that they got up and walked out.

Dyanne: We used to do all of the weddings at the Starship Enterprise re-creation at the Hilton here in Las Vegas. They used to often have Nimoy and Shatner there signing autographs at the same time as us, but they were so busy they never even got a chance to say anything. It was just constant signing by both of them.

Howie: At $150 a signature.

What is the strangest thing you have been asked to autograph?
Dyanne: A 15-month-old baby's foot. The parents were so proud they immediately started photographing it.

What is the most inappropriate thing a fan has done or said to you?
Dyanne: Never at any show. The people there are great.

Howie: Dyanne had a stalker once.

Dyanne: That was when I was doing a comedy revue here in Las Vegas with Tim Conway from *The Carol Burnett Show*. I was doing sketch comedy. Steve Lawrence and Edie Gormé were in the show too. I started getting these phone calls and they turned into death threats. It got to the point where S.W.A.T. had to come and clear our house.

What about the flipside? What is the sweetest or most touching thing a fan has said or done for you?
Dyanne: There are too many to name. We have met so many wonderful people and received so many accolades. I guess my favorites were this couple from Sweden. The woman was pregnant at the time and she was asking us about buying souvenirs from our website, but instead we insisted on giving them a gift. They ended up having

a little girl and naming her Tillie Ilsa. We still keep in touch with them.

Do fans ever get physical with you or invade your personal space?
Howie: Not our fans.

Dyanne: Never. Not a problem.

Howie: Dyanne, as a minister, has performed many wedding ceremonies for various motorcycle gangs, and you will never see anyone treat anyone else with more respect than they do my Dyanne.

Dyanne: If anyone makes a sound, they get up and throw their colleague out.

Howie: Of course, everyone knows not to mess with Ilsa. She's an expert marksman.

Dyanne: Every Halloween I go to the shooting range and then nail my shot out human shaped targets on my door, and they all have bullet holes in the head, heart and groin.

Have you taken part in any cast reunions of any of your films at conventions?
Howie: We can't. Everyone is dead.

Dyanne: We did a few shows with Don Edmonds before he died. He was the director *of Ilsa :She Wolf of the SS.* We also do shows with Bill Moseley from time to time. The three of us were in *The House of the Witch Doctor.*

When I was at the Calgary comic book convention, a 400-pound guy stepped on my foot and I yelled out "Jesus Christ!" A cosplayer dressed as Jesus Christ (at least I think it was a cosplayerg) promptly appeared and offered to heal me. What is your personal WTF story from any convention?
Howard: It was at a show in Tampa. Two nuns came up to me and they were the most swect, most complimentary young ladies I have ever met. I offered to give them autographed photos for free and they insisted on paying. Then they turned around and I saw that the entire rear halves of

their bodies were naked. I thought they were real nuns! As they walked off, I yelled at them, "Don't get in the habit of doing that!"

Dyanne: Wasn't that the same show where the Japanese guy knew you?
Howie: No, that was a different one. But anyway, this Japanese guy came up to me, and said, "You write songs? I love your song," and I was puzzled, because I do write songs, but hadn't mentioned it at this show.

Dyanne: He remembered Howie from a seminar he had spoken at in Japan years previous.

Howie: I worked in Japan for a while. I sang in a commercial for a cologne that's the Japanese version of Old Spice. The producers asked me to change one line and re-record it, but instead I ended up rewriting the whole song and Jerry Wallace recorded it. Then, the song from the commercial got released as a single in Japan too. I still get royalties. It went to #1 four different times.

What experiences have you had with fans who know far more about your characters than you could ever hope to know? How do you deal with that situation?
Howie: It is constant. Dyed-in-the-wool fans know everything.

Dyanne: They remember names of characters and films I forgot from years ago. It was actually some fans who told me that *Blood Sabbath* had been released. That movie was cursed. The producer died during production. We had three different cinematographers because the first two got so freaked out that they quit. There were money problems and I ended up not getting paid everything I was promised. They finally hired a voodoo princess to come in and cleanse the set. I only learned it was released years later because some fans brought me a VHS copy to sign.

Howie: One time some people wanted to buy a movie that doesn't exist.

Dyanne: It's true! Two guys came up to us at a show and wanted to buy the movie I made with Bruce Lee! They read a review of it on the internet and thought it sounded so bad it would be funny. Now I did study karate once, and I was supposed to make a movie with the man who took over for Bruce Lee after he died, but the movie was never made. And somebody wrote a review about it anyway, and said I was horrible in it!

Howie: You can't always trust reviews. One time three different people reviewed my nightclub act. They were all at the same performance. Two of them said it was the best show they had ever seen, and one said it was the worst. I found out later that the guy who hated it got so drunk he fell asleep before I even started and never saw a second of it.

Do fans ever come up to you imitating one of your own characters?
Dyanne: No, but I have been given footage of people recreating Ilsa scenes for acting classes, including one famous actress I won't name but who used Ilsa as a model for playing a dominant woman.

Howie: We've been given a couple of movies made by Ilsa lookalikes.

Dyanne: One was from Bulgaria and one was from Switzerland. I know the girls will turn into wonderful actresses, but right now those movies are only good for laughs. They walk like they are models on a catwalk. It's like watching a baby trying to imitate a fifty-year-old.

You both have an extensive background in comedy. Do you approach fans with a sense of humor?
Howie: Always. If fans want to be serious, we'll be serious, but it's not our first choice.

Dyanne: We love doing Q and A's at shows. They are usually the best part. Howie has lots of great stories to tell. Tell him some of your stories about *Ilsa, Tigress of Siberia*.

Howie: They did this one shot where a guy is being hung upside down into this freezing cold lake. They had to hire a Navy SEAL to do the stunt. We were told we had no choice but to do it in one take because if it took two, he'd die. On that same movie, I had to ride a horse. I had never been on a horse in my life. Every time I got on it, he found a new way to buck me off. In one scene, they offered to give me a stunt double, but I said why bother? He'd already thrown me off every way possible. I was wrong.

It was the big scene in the movie, and he threw me right over his head. Luckily, we were shooting in a blizzard and snow was halfway up his legs and I wasn't hurt.

What celebrity encounters have you had at conventions? Feel free to tell us any funny, sexy and/or terrifying close encounters you have had.

Dyanne: We were speaking at a fan film festival in New York. We had dinner with this fan club and talked to them afterwards and it was great. At these things, you meet a lot of people and forget most of them. It turned out that one of the people we met was an agent, and he went back to his agency and told two other agents about these two great actors he met at this dinner.

Howie: So we get back to Las Vegas, and Dyanne gets this call from an agent she's never met to come interview for a film. And then I get a call from an agent I've never met to come interview for a film.

Dyanne: But it was two different people, and the interviews were in two different locations.

Howie: So then Dyanne gets a call and is told she's going to play a bride in this movie. Then I get a call and I turn to her and say, "I'm going to play your groom."

Dyanne: We had only been married about a year, so we wore the clothes from our own wedding!

Howie: So, two days later we show up to be in this movie, and the actor who was supposed to play the minister didn't show up, so the director quickly filled in for him.

Dyanne: The director was Robert Altman, and the movie was *Aria*. We have it on DVD.

Have you ever been mistaken for someone else at a convention, and thought "why the Hell did you think I was them?"

Howie: Barbara Eden. Dyanne can't go to a show or hotel without people thinking she is Barbara Eden.

Dyanne: For Howie it is Christopher Walken. He goes somewhere and people think it's Christopher Walken doing the show or a Christopher Walken lookalike. Tell him about the funeral you did.

Howie: I got called to do a funeral for someone only a year after I had married him. A lot of the same people who went to the wedding went to the funeral. Somebody said, "Christopher! You came back!" I said the reason I was 10 minutes late was that I knew a lot of people from Fox were going to be there and I left my Christopher Walken audition tape in the car.

Cosplay has become an art form. What costume at any convention has totally blown you away and amazed you with its high quality and detail? What is the all-time worst costume you have seen?

Howie: The best ones are the ones that use stilts. It takes a lot of talent to get around in them.

OK, now it's all you: What is the one knock-'em-dead, blow-their-socks-off fan convention story that you haven't told us yet? It can be funny, sad, scary, sexy, heart-warming, terrifying, sexy, action packed, cerebral, sexy or gross. Did I mention it could be sexy?

Dyanne: There are too many. We were doing a show in Cleveland and the son of the producer of Ilsa came and gave me a portrait of me as Ilsa that his dad had commissioned. He said we could keep it or auction it or do whatever we wanted with it.

Howie: It's appraised at $20,000. I said auction it.

Dyanne: And I told you that's not going to happen. Ever. We also have a smaller version of it that's been appraised at $10,000. Our home is full of pictures and gifts that I've gotten since I started being Ilsa. One fan we met is Don Edwards who is now a famous artist and he has sent us pictures from all of our productions. One time we were in Paris and we met the head of the Academy of Art in Paris, Jean Pierre Combes. He still sends us mail with these beautiful paintings he does on the envelopes. We knew an artist who was trained in the concentration camps and did a great portrait of me. I have lots of Ilsa dolls people have made. I have a beautiful she-wolf plaque that someone made and gave me. Fans have brought me lingerie.

Lots of times people make all this effort to make and bring me a gift and then they run away without talking to me.

Howie: We know Mike Natarelli. He's a tattoo artist and glazier. He made us glassware with our pictures on them. They are amazing likenesses. Sometimes people give us pictures we didn't even know had been taken of us. We have met so many great people.

Dyanne: We were in Belgium doing voiceover work and we were driven to Holland for a prepared showing. Howie and I were each given 10 words in Dutch to say to the audience. As soon as we walked on stage, everyone stood up. I looked around to see if the Pope was behind me.

Howie: That was great. We stayed after the movie was shown to sign autographs, to shake hands, and everyone kept coming up and saying, "Love you." Tell him about the little boy in Paris.

Dyanne: We were invited to this party in Paris by this amazing lady who spoke all kinds of languages, but her son only spoke French. She gave me a photograph that I admired hanging on her wall and everyone at the party signed it. Her son signed his name and the only English word he knew: love.

But the best gift I ever got from anyone is a song Howie wrote for me. He'll send it to you to put in your book. It's about me being an actress, but it's how every woman wants to think their man thinks about them.

Howie: Hey, when you're married to Ilsa, you take every precaution possible!

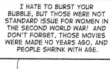

EVERYONE WANTS A PIECE OF THE PIE: A TRUE STORY STARRING DYANNE THORNE

WHEN I WAS LIVING IN LOS ANGELES, I'D OFTEN GO TO A CERTAIN RESTAURANT FOR A CHEAP, QUICK SUPPER. THEY SOLD PIZZA BY THE SLICE.

THE FOOD WAS GOOD, AND A LOT OF ACTORS ATE THERE BECAUSE IT WAS CLOSE TO ONE OF THE STUDIOS.

ONE OF THE ACTORS WHO WORKED AT THAT STUDIO WAS BURT LANCASTER. ONE NIGHT HE ENDED UP SITTING DIRECTLY ACROSS FROM ME. I WAS SO STAR-STRUCK I COULDN'T CHEW, LET ALONE TALK TO HIM.

I DID MANAGE TO WRITE HIM A SHORT NOTE TELLING HIM ABOUT OUR CLOSE ENCOUNTER

I DID MANAGE TO WRITE HIM A SHORT NOTE TELLING HIM ABOUT OUR CLOSE ENCOUNTER

MR. LANCASATER IS GLAD THAT YOU ENJOYED YOUR PIZZA.

FROM HIS SECRETARY.

Larry Thomas

Larry Thomas played Osama Bin Laden in *Postal* in 2007, yet, strangely enough, that is neither the scariest nor the craziest character he has ever played. In 1995, Larry Thomas entered pop culture history when he stole the show as the Soup Nazi in the most popular episode of the most popular sitcom ever, *Seinfeld*.

In addition to creating one of the most famous catchphrases ever, he has more than 65 IMDb credits and is one of the hardest-working and most in-demand stage actors and directors around. He is constantly in demand as he criss-crosses North America to appear in independent films and stage productions. His intense schedule made it impossible to find time to answer more than three questions for this book, and even that took months to arrange. Therefore, if you ever get a chance to see him at a fan convention, make sure you go see him. Trust me, there are other places he could be, and he is making a real effort to meet you, the fans he loves.

For convenience, Larry Thomas now comes in a handy travel size.

Can you give us a quick list of the fan conventions you have appeared at, as both a fan and celebrity guest?
Hollywood show, Chiller Theatre, Niagara Falls, Salt Lake City, Rhode Island, Houston Comicpalooza, TVland, San Jose, National sports convention, Toronto Fan Fest, Wizard World in Anaheim, NY, Austin, Philly. Wondercon, San Diego comic con, Adventure con, Steel City con...

What is the sweetest or most touching thing a fan has said or done for you?
That the humor of Seinfeld helped their dad through Chemo.

Before you became a celebrity you were a fan. Ever have any true fanboy moments encountering celebrities before you became one?
I have had a few encounters but the funniest was seeing Cary Grant on the street in Beverly Hills. I totally planned to tell him how much I loved him but as I approached him I must have blacked out because the next thing I knew I was alone and I turned and he was walking away. I'll never know if I said anything or not. Also, I once saw Dustin Hoffman on a plane with his wife, Lisa. I blurted out to him, "You are such a genius!" He replied, "Tell that to my wife." It was pretty funny.

Helene Udy

Helene Udy is best known for her recurring role (74 episodes) on the long-running *Dr Quinn, Medicine Woman* television series, but she also has genuine cult movie star status for her impeccable horror résumé which includes *The Dead Zone, Amityville: Evil Never Dies, Stirring, House of Demons, First House on the Hill, The Last Revenants, Swamp Freak* and *3 Wicked Witches*. At conventions, she most often is part of a cast reunion for one of her first films, the cult classic *My Bloody Valentine*. Helene's character Sylvia was not the lead of the movie, but her death is definitely the most memorable.

Among *Star Trek* fans she is famous for being the first woman to play a Ferengi but has never been invited to a *Star Trek* convention. Get with it, Trekkies!

In addition to acting and convention appearances, Helene keeps busy with her business, www.createaparty.com.

If there was ever an actor who loves her fans as much they love her, it is Helene. Seek her out at the next convention she is at and expect a hug.

Part of Helene's famous death scene. It gets worse from here.

Can you give us a quick list of the fan conventions you have appeared at, as both a fan and celebrity guest?
Cinema Wasteland, Bay of Blood, Scream Queens, Monster Mania, and others.

What is the strangest thing you have been asked to autograph?

Someone wanted an autographed photo of my foot. They didn't specify my left or right foot. I don't keep photos of my feet on hand, so I didn't give them one.

What is the most inappropriate thing a fan has done or said to you?

Nothing really comes to mind. Horror fans are the sweetest people in the world, and I mainly do horror shows.

I was doing a movie once and there was one production assistant who was turning into a stalker. It got to the point where they stopped calling him into work.

What about the flipside? What is the sweetest or most touching thing a fan has said or done for you?

Become my friend. Some of my friends started out as being fans. They are incredibly supportive and very interesting people.

In terms of an individual fan, the sweetest and most unexpected gift I have received from a fan was my own mutilated corpse. It was the dummy that had been used for my death scene in *My Bloody Valentine*. A fan had bought it online and was keeping it for me until they had a chance to meet me. They gave it to me at a show in Toronto. I donated it to a noted horror collector because an artifact like that takes some expertise to care for.

Do fans ever get physical with you or invade your personal space?

Never. I get physical with my fans. I always hug them. I feel safe around people who have made an effort to travel just to meet me. I want to greet them properly. I have never had a problem.

You are best known for your recurring role on the hit show Dr. Quinn, Medicine Woman. Do they come out to see you?

Dr. Quinn fans don't do conventions, and they only want to meet Jane Seymour. Maybe once every 10 years some fans will organize a lunch and the old cast members will go. But we don't sign autographs or do photo ops or anything. We just eat lunch.

When I was at the Calgary comic book convention, a 400 pound guy stepped on my foot and I yelled out "Jesus Christ!" A cosplayer dressed as Jesus Christ

(at least I think it was a cosplayer) promptly appeared and offered to heal me. What is your personal WTF story from any convention?

I am always surprised that the fans are so interested in killers. The victims may be the main characters in the movie, but they want to know about the killers, especially the miner in *My Bloody Valentine.*

What experiences have you had with fans who know far more about your characters than you could ever hope to know? How do you deal with that situation?

All of the fans know more than I do. Horror fans aren't like other fans. They will watch a movie over and over. I don't do that. I haven't even seen the remake.

Do fans ever come up to you imitating one of your own characters?

Nobody comes to a horror convention dressed like one of the victims.

What celebrity encounters have you had at conventions? Feel free to tell us any funny, sexy and/or terrifying close encounters you have had.

When I was just starting out in New York, I used to go to the Café Central on the west side. You would see Sean Penn, Madonna, Chris Reeve, people like that. I used to hang out with a lot of celebrities, but those stories are personal. Celebrities are people too.

Have you ever been mistaken for someone else at a convention, and thought "why the Hell did you think I was them?

Lori Hallier, the star of *My Bloody Valentine.* It happens all the time because we're at the same shows and we're both small and blonde. I was mistaken for Courtney Cox once, and I have no idea why. We look nothing alike. I'm blonde and she's brunette.

Are horror fans surprised you were also a western star?

No, it's the opposite. Western fans don't understand why I do horror. If someone comes to me with an interesting project, I'm going to do it. I've been lucky to do horror films because I've had a chance to work with brilliant people. George Mihalka, who directed *My Bloody Valentine* is an underrated genius. Like a lot of Canadian artists, he has trouble getting the proper credit.

Cosplay has become an art form. What costume at any convention has totally blown you away and amazed you with its high quality and detail? What is the all-time worst costume you have seen?

I have seen so many that none really stand out. Lots of the miner ones are very good. There are no bad costumes. Fans are amazing people, and if they have gone to the trouble to come in costume, that's good enough for me.

Gender bender cosplay continues to get more and more popular. Have you met a male version of one of your characters at conventions? What was that like?

Never for one of my characters.

You have been interviewed and done panels at conventions. What are the funniest, strangest and most thought provoking questions you have encountered?

I have taken part in many *My Bloody Valentine* panels. The most common questions I get are about my death scene, like how it was shot, and what was going through my mind at the time. I was 16 at the time and took acting very seriously, so I managed to convince myself as well as the audience that I was dying.

You are often on the road. What is the hardest part about travel?

None! I love being on the road! I've gone right across this country and once did a movie in France. I love meeting new people, seeing new sights, exploring new places, learning new languages. Take me on the road right now if you can!

OK, now it's all you: What is the one knock-'em-dead, blow-their-socks-off fan convention story that you haven't told us yet? It can be funny, sad, scary, sexy, heart-warming, terrifying, sexy, action packed, cerebral, sexy or gross.

The most memorable one is the saddest one. At the last show he did, Alf Humphries, who played Howard in *My Bloody Valentine,* told us that he had dementia. It turned out that he had undiagnosed brain cancer and he died shortly thereafter. Nobody expected it. His wife was wonderful and made sure that he got to the show, and I and the rest of the cast were so incredibly grateful for that. It is always horrible when a member of that cast dies. We became so close. Even now, I feel like I could call on any of them for help if I needed it. Cherish your friends. We take people for granted. Hug your friends.

IF HELENE UDY HAD PLAYED MYRA BING IN MY BLOODY VALENTINE

ALF HUMPHRIES 1953-2018

Mike Watt

Writer, director, and journalist Mike Watt wrote and directed *THE RESURRECTION GAME* (2001) and Bloody Earth Film's *A FEAST OF FLESH* (2007) (aka "Abattoir") through Happy Cloud Pictures, which he co-founded with the lovely and talented Amy Lynn Best and the less lovely but also talented Bill Homan. He also wrote the screenplays for *SEVERE INJURIES* (2003), *WERE-GRRL* (2002), *SPLATTER MOVIE: THE DIRECTOR'S CUT* (2008), *DEAD MEN WALKING* (2005) for The Asylum, *THE SCREENING* (2007) for G. Cameron Romero, as well as *DEMON DIVAS AND THE LANES OF DAMNATION* (2009) and *RAZOR DAYS* (2015). Mike has worked as an editor, producer, actor, and most any other job needed to complete a film or short. He was the editor of *Sirens of Cinema Magazine* and is, in his own words "always tirelessly pursuing most anything to pay his rent… ah, further the independent film spirit and camaraderie all of us in this business equally share."

Can you give us a quick list of the fan conventions you have appeared at, as both a fan and celebrity guest?
We've been doing shows for 25 years and a lot of come and gone. Amy Lynn Best and I have been official guests at Cinema Wasteland since 2002. Horror Realm in Pittsburgh put us as valued guests. Twisted Nightmare Weekend, The Haunted Hotel Convention, Dark X-Mas, The Pittsburgh Comicon, Flashback Weekend, the first Days of the Dead, and Fangoria Weekend of Horrors, not to mention at least a dozen more single-day, single shot cons. We've attended Monster Mania, Chiller, Horrorhound, on a regular basis for many years as well. We also ran Genghis Con in Pittsburgh 2006-2007.

What is the most inappropriate thing a fan has done or said to you?
"Why are you here? I thought all the guests were famous."

    My response: "Who paid to get in? Wasn't me."

What about the flipside? What is the sweetest or most touching thing a fan has said or done for you?
We had a magnificent man named Tim Buccholtz who became a de facto Happy Cloud producer who would send Amy wonderful birthday gifts and even paid our way to a Fangoria Show. Another fan carved a couple of beautiful pumpkins depicting Amy from one of our films.

Have you had people come up to you dressed as one of the characters from your movies?
Even the people in our movies don't come dressed as characters from our movies.

When I was at the Calgary comic book convention, a 400 pound guy stepped on my foot and I yelled out "Jesus Christ!" A cosplayer dressed as Jesus Christ (at least I think it was a cosplayer) promptly appeared and offered to heal me. What is your personal WTF story from any convention?

After-hours at Cinema Wasteland, the show moves to the bar and lobby area. About 2am, a roving band of bagpipers showed up out of nowhere to play "Amazing Grace".

What experiences have you had with fans who know far more about your career than you could ever hope to know? How do you deal with that situation?

Amy had a guy who insistently changed her birthplace on her IMDb page, no matter how many times she clarified it for him. I had another "fan" accuse me in print of being a "convicted child molester" that caused me enormous problems back in 2007. There is no way to deal with strange fans. The more aggressive ones get police calls. These are two very extreme and rare exceptions.

What other celebrity encounters have you had at conventions? Feel free to tell us any funny, sexy and/or terrifying close encounters you have had.

Far too many to recount. I wrote three books detailing the strange and wonderful encounters I've had with celebrities. A great many of them became personal friends. Every year we raise a glass to the departed (and genuinely wonderful) Gunnar Hansen, Ted V. Mikels, Herschel Gordon Lewis - all of whom did us tremendous favors.

Have you ever been mistaken for someone else at a convention, and thought "why the Hell did you think I was them?"

No. People still think it's funny to "mistake" me for Mike Watt the bassist, but I got the last word when he wrote the intro to one of my books.

Cosplay has become an art form. What costume at nay convention has totally blown you away and amazed you with its high quality and detail? What is the all-time worst costume you have seen?

I don't know what the "worst" is. If you want to come in costume, who am I to criticize. Some of the best I saw at San Diego Comic Con, but the better ones showed up at Horrorfind and Horror Realm - costumes based on the player's own imagination rather than trying to duplicate someone else's characters.

You have been photographed thousands of times. What is your favorite photo with a fan, and what was the one request that made you shake your head, laugh or throw up a little in your mouth?

I'm actually photographed very little at these things. Amy is the face of the company and most people are extremely respectful with photo requests. One guy who made the comic con rounds liked to slowly lower his hand while the photo was taken, but Amy and the other women present put a stop to that.

Before you became a celebrity you were a fan. Ever have any true fangirl moments encountering celebrities before you became one?

I had a momentary loss of verbal eloquence when I met Neil Gaiman in person, despite having interviewed him several times prior to publication of *AMERICAN GODS*. Our biz partner, Bill Homan, and I once posed as college students to worm our way into a meeting with Steve Whitmire while he was still with the Muppets. The worst experience I ever had, outside of journalist interviews, was when I met Julian Sands and his entire filmography went completely out of my head. I drew an utter blank on his non-genre career and blew the entire conversation. I can't think of anyone rude or nasty to me in person. Steve Railsback and I talked for three hours about *THE STUNT MAN*, pausing only to sign for fans.

You have been interviewed and done panels at conventions. What are the funniest, strangest and most thought provoking questions you have encountered?

Well, I discovered a co-panelist was a white supremacist during a conversation, that was fun. Most of the panels I wind up on don't get more than a couple of attendees. On panels with more experienced writers, I don't have much to say. With less experienced writers, I don't get to say anything.

Have you done any foreign conventions yet?

We did a show in Canada but were lost in the throngs. We screened *RAZOR DAYS* and it did very well, but we didn't do much in the way of sales once Shatner and Patrick Stewart arrived for their photo ops.

You are constantly on the road. What is the hardest part about travel, and your funniest story from being on the road?

Every convention is little more than highways and hotels for us. We rarely see the outside world during the 2-3 days of the show. Coming back from one event, we got caught in a blizzard on the highway and did a 360 in heavy traffic. Not sure if that's "funny", but fortunately it was our last show of the year. Although there was the time we were driving through Manhattan and almost ran over Parker Posey who crossed against the light in front of us. That would have made "For Your Consideration" awkward.

CPSIA information can be obtained
at www.ICGtesting.com
Printed in the USA
JSHW032137280722
28676JS00007B/226